Prayers, Poems
& Precious Moments

Mary J Bryant

This Book is
Dedicated to
LaTonya S. Wilson Barker

Mary J. Bryant

ISBN – 9780-578-13238-9
Library of Congress Control Number 2013956302

Printed in USA
Reprint 2017

Photography – Vic Newton, 2026 Photography
Cover Design – LōMar Designs
Beauty Consultant – Janell Bryant
Makeup Artist – Chrissy Woods
Hair – SaTonya Bryant, Anointed Hands Hair Salon
Accessories – Alice Walker, 4 Ever Shopping

This Book Belongs to

,

Dedication

This book is dedicated to my husband Michael Anthony of 31 years, my sons Michael Anthony, Jr. and Marquis Jarod, my daughter Megan Janell and my granddaughter Michaela Jayne Grace. They have been my inspiration from the conception of writing this book. I have gotten encouragement during those times when I was discouraged. I praise God for them.

I acknowledge the support of Gerald Seals, mentor and teacher. I acknowledge Louise Smith who has taken me under her wings in getting this book project off the ground and running. (Thanks for that awesome breakfast and fellowship).

Last, but not least, I thank God the Father, God the Son and God the Holy Spirit for the good work that He has started in me. As Psalm 37:3-6 states: Trust in the Lord and do good, dwell in the land and enjoy safe pasture. Take delight in the Lord, and he will give you the desires of your heart. Commit your way to the Lord; trust in him and he will do this: He will make your righteous reward shine like the dawn, your vindication like the noonday sun.

In God's Hands & His Service,
Mary J. Bryant,
Servant of the Most High God

Prayers, Poems & Precious Moments

TABLE OF CONTENTS

DEDICATION 4

FOREWORD 8

INTRODUCTION 9

PRAYERS 10

WALKING IN UNITY 12

THIRSTY FOR THE LORD IN THE TIME OF TROUBLE............................ 14

THE LORD IS MY SOVEREIGN LORD 15

SEEKING AN AWESOME GOD WITH THANKSGIVING.......................... 16

AND PRAISE.. 16

CHANGING FROM THE INSIDE OUT 18

LEAD ME IN YOUR RIGHTEOUSNESS...................................... 20

STRENGTHEN ME AS I WALK BY FAITH AND NOT FEELINGS 21

I TURN TO THE LOVER OF MY SOUL, JESUS. 22

A PRAYER WHILE IN DISTRESS... 23

A FOLLOW UP TO THE PRAYER OF DISTRESS 24

BURDENED, BURNED OUT, BEWILDERED 26

GREAT EXPECTATIONS!.. 28

WOMAN AFTER GOD'S HEART 29

"HIS EYE IS ON THE SPARROW" 32

GOD ALONE 34

GOD'S MERCY DOES ENDURES FOREVER 36

HOUSE OF HONOR 38

OFF WITH THE OLD AND ON WITH THE NEW 42

PRAYING FOR REVELATION KNOWLEDGE 44

PRESSING MY WAY THROUGH IT ALL..................................... 48

RESTING IN HIS ABSOLUTE GOODNESS 50

POEMS... 51

Fully God, Fully Man... 52

You 54

Alone with My Jesus 57

Just Jesus! 59

My Heart's Desire.. 61

My Soul Yearns... 63

Oh How Sweet 65

Through His Eyes.. 66

PRECIOUS MOMENTS 68

YOU ARE WORTHY LORD 70

WONDERFUL JESUS! 71

THE LORD HAS DONE GREAT THINGS........................... 72

MY DAILY BREAD.. 74

OVERWHELMED IN HIS PRESENCE 75

MORE OF JESUS AND LESS OF ME 76

I LOVE HIM BECAUSE HE FIRST LOVE ME....................... 78

JESUS, MORE THAN ENOUGH.................................... 79

TIMES OF REFRESHING 81

ALONE WITH YOU 83

CAUGHT UP IN HIS LOVE 85

ONLY BY HIS GOODNESS.. 87

I AM THE APPLE OF HIS EYE....................................... 88

RIVERS OF LIVING WATER: SEEK, KNOCK, ASK................. 89

THAT'S GOOD NEWS 90

REVERENCE TO A HOLY GOD...................................... 92

THE LOVE OF THE LORD LEAVES ME SPEECHLESS 94

NO ONE CAN LOVE ME LIKE JESUS! 95

SURRENDERED TO HIS WILL: UNDER RECONSTRUCTION 96

REALIZATION BECAUSE OF REVELATION 98

YEARNING TO BE IN HIS PRESENCE.............................. 99

BE STILL 100

JUST FOR WHO YOU ARE... 101

HUMBLED BECAUSE OF WHO HE IS 102

MY PRAISE OUTWEIGHS MY PAIN 103

HE DESERVES THE GLORY, THE HONOR AND THE PRAISE 104

SECRET PLACE 107

BROUGHT OUT TO BE BROUGHT IN: OUT OF DARKNESS INTO HIS

MARVELOUS LIGHT 109

GIVER OF EVERY GOOD AND PERFECT GIFT.................................... 111

WHEN TRUTH MEETS ERROR.. 112

WHEN NOTHING ELSE WILL DO 114

THERE IS WISDOM IN THE FEAR OF THE LORD................................. 117

MY SHEPHERD 119

MORNING AFTER MORNING NEW MERCIES COME........................... 121

KEEPING THE LORD EVER BEFORE ME.. 123

COME JESUS!.. 125

THE CAPACITY TO GROW IN GRACE 128

HELP ME JESUS! HEAR MY HEART'S DESIRE.................................... 130

THE TRUTH AND NOTHING BUT THE TRUTH 131

ENCOMPASSED BY HIS PRESENCE 133

THE LORD IS MY DELIGHT 134

SOMEWHERE LISTENING FOR HIS VOICE 135

Foreword

Dear Reader, as you read *Prayer, Poems & Precious Moments* you will experience Sister Bryant's journey to a deeper relationship with God. Her willingness to share her most intimate thoughts, forebodings, and joys with God is personally enriching. When you get midpoint of your reading, you, as did I, may exclaim "This dear sister has the relationship with God that I desire! She trusts God!" It was at that point when I closed the book and took a few moments to engage in contemplation. The familiar words of Psalm 23:1, "The Lord is my shepherd, I shall not want," rolled around in my mind. Inspired by Sister Bryant's contemplative pacing, I mulled over the thoughts:

"It is the Lord Himself who shepherds me. He is my Shepherd at all times, in every situation, no matter my activity or circumstance. Even though He is the shepherd for others, He, my Shepherd, knows me and I know Him. He is my ever present help. Therefore, I do not want."

I then reopened the book and started reading it from the beginning. Now, I am more aware that while reading Bryant's intimate talks with Our Father I realize that my desire is to continually have a deeper relationship with God. I have that relationship not because of my actions but because he relates to me in love. I love him and want to be like Jesus. I believe you will experience the same and your prayer life will reflect the enrichment.

Pastor Gerald Seals
Living Word Church & Fellowship of Our Lord and Savior Jesus Christ

Introduction

"We love him, because he first loved us."
(1 John 4:19)

Realizing God sent His Son Jesus to die for me, I have decided to follow His way. My life has been redeemed from destruction. He has crowned me with loving kindness and tender mercies (Psalm 103). God's great love towards me has made me pursue the very lover and sustainer of my soul – the LORD my God.

Through the years, my relationship with Christ has grown tremendously. His love for me, along with faith and obedience, are keys to a maturing and sustaining relationship with God. His love has taken me from mountain to mountain and from valley to valley, and I would not change one moment of what I have gained and am still gaining in the process.

There have been days when I was so low I could barely lift my eyes towards heaven to cry for help. Yet there have been days when I was on top of the mountain not wanting to come down from the presence of my Abba, Father.

I personally believe that God longs for His children to show an external expression of an internal commitment to Him. We should live a life of love, faith and obedience that inspires us to live passionately for Him and not passively to ourselves.

My union and communion with God have inspired wonderful journal entries, which I call *Prayers, Poems, & Precious Moments*, that only the Holy Spirit could have created through a woman after God's own heart. It has indeed been a supernaturally incredible journey thus far, and I want to share some of those passages with you; and maybe, just maybe, you will be inspired to grow closer to Jesus in your own personal way.

In God's Hands and His Service,
Mary J. Bryant

*P*rayers

"But as for me, my prayer is to you, Yahweh, in an acceptable time. God, in the abundance of your loving kindness, answer me in the truth of your salvation." (Psalms 69:14)

"From the end of the earth, I will call to you, when my heart is overwhelmed. Lead me to the rock that is higher than I." (Psalm 61:2)

Prayer for me was and is essential in my walk and relationship with God the Father, God the Son and God the Holy Spirit. The importance of a constant and consistent prayer life cannot be overstated. I can attest that prayer is my lifeline to heaven.

I have learned and experienced the feeling of confusion and being overwhelmed when I go without praying for any length of time. Even with Jesus and the Holy Spirit as our Intercessors, prayer is much needed to keep connected to the Father.

With life's challenges and those things that just drains us can make our hearts and minds feel weary and worn out. It can even make us feel like giving up. As spirit beings, we have spiritual needs for nourishment and refreshment. Prayer gives us that strength and renewal in our spirits. Jesus also needed that time to be renewed and refreshed. So if the Son of God needed it while He was on earth; surely we too need it all the more.

So, find your place in God with prayer and start your life to connecting with your Father Who created you.

But he answered, "It is written, 'Man shall not live by bread alone, but by every word that proceeds out of the mouth of God. (Matthew 4:4)

Jesus' disciples saw the many miracles He performed but the thing that they asked Him was to teach them to pray: "When he finished praying in a certain place, one of his disciples said to him, "Lord, teach us to pray, just as John also taught his disciples." (Luke 11:2)

Walking in Unity

"Lord, open my lips. My mouth shall declare your praise."
(Psalm 51:15)

ur Father, my continued prayer is that our hearts are always open to you. May we seek your kingdom and righteousness with all faithfulness, zeal and diligence. May we become a people who worship you in spirit and in truth. May you saturate us with your abundant love, and allow that love to flow, one from another. If we love one another, the world will see this and know that we are your disciples.

I pray that you give your people a heart to serve others. Guide us with your unfailing love. Protect us from all harm and lead us in your everlasting way. The world has to be able to see you in us. Help us Lord to be true Disciples of Christ.

From the depth of my belly I cry out to you Father, for us - the church– the body of Christ—to walk in unity. I cry out to you for your truth to be told in all fullness nothing added or taken away. I cry to you for us to have a hunger and thirst for your Word, your truth, your Presence, your glory.

Oh bless you Father. I praise you. We give thanks to you as our heavenly and holy Father. Teach us to enter more deeply into the mystery of the church, that it may be more effective for us and for the world. Help us to seek your kingdom first in all we do. Teach us so our hearts will hunger and thirst for Christ, more and more, until we overflow from the fountain of living water.

As we walk in your light, may we fellowship with each other so that the world will see you in us and know you are God. As we see others in need, may we reach out with the love of Christ by the Holy Spirit. As we teach the truth of your word, may we receive revelation knowledge of the mysteries of the church. We are the sheep of your pasture. Feed us from the Bread of Life.

Mary J. Bryant

Thirsty for the Lord in the Time of Trouble

*"I sought Yahweh, and he answered me, and delivered me
from all my fears." (Psalm 34:4)*

Father, even when it seems as though my troubles are like death to my soul, you deliver me, and dry my tears. I am encouraged that you care about me. You are my salvation. I thirst for your righteousness. Lord, I will offer you the sacrifice of thanksgiving and praise.

Continue to teach me your truth and show me your way. Help me to keep my mind focus on you and not my troubles. Revive me with your Spirit because I am afflicted. You are my hiding place. My hope is in your Word.

Lord, I have experienced your goodness in the time of my distress. Your ears were open to my cry for help. I trust in you. Deliver me according to the power of your love. My heart yearns for you like a deer yearns for water. Come to me in this place of trouble. Let the rivers of living water flow through me. I give you glory, praise and honor.

Thank you for meeting me right where I was. In Jesus name I do pray. Amen!

The Lord is My Sovereign LORD

"Without faith it is impossible to be well pleasing to him, for he who comes to God must believe that he exists, and that he is a rewarder of those who seek him."
(Hebrews 11:6)

Father, I thank you for being a faithful God. I thank you that your promises are yes and amen. I thank you that you are not like man that you should lie and your word will not return void. You will perform what your word says according to what is pleasing to you. I thank you for knowing what is best for me. Father, I praise you for your awesome power and your wonderful works. I adore you. I am in awe of you. I reverence you for you are Sovereign. You are everlasting and eternal. You were before time existed. You knew the end even before the beginning. Nothing is hidden from you. Your power is matchless. Your glory is majestic. Oh how sweet is the sound of your name to my ears. Oh how precious is your name to my mouth. I worship you. As I learn of you, I grow stronger and stronger and closer and closer to you. I am decreasing while you are increasing. I thirst for you, fill me up. Your Holy Spirit anoints me with power to do your will. Your word equips me with your truth. I fall on my knees with my face bowed down before you. I am humbled beneath your mighty and powerful hands. Teach me your ways. Direct and order my steps, lead me into your everlasting way. I am weak, but you are strong. I seek your face. Please don't hide your face from me. Shine on your servant daughter. Help me to complete the work you have assigned to me so that I too can say "it is finished". I want to hear you say well done my good and faithful servant. Welcome home. In Jesus name I pray, Amen.

Mary J. Bryant

Seeking an Awesome God with Thanksgiving and Praise

"Praise Yahweh, my soul, and don't forget all his benefits"
(Psalm 103:2)

Heavenly Father I thank you for being my helper. Thank you for encouraging me. Thank you for being an on time God. Thank you for being mighty and powerful. Thank you that no problem life throws at me, no heartache, no disappointment, and no demon in hell can snatch me from your righteous right hand. Thank you that you are able to keep me from falling. Knowing all things work together for good for them that love the Lord who are the called according to His purpose. I am so blessed because of your love, your goodness, your grace, your mercy, your compassion, and your good favor towards me. I am so rich in my soul because you came and fellowship with me. I bask in your glory! Thank **YOU** dear Father for coming to see about me and to let me know I am yours. Although my weeping may last for a while, I don't despair because joy will come.

I am so grateful to you. How do I leave this place with you? I feel like Enoch probably felt, walking and talking with you. For I desire to live a godly life before you, one that is pleasing in your sight. I never want to offend you with what I say or do. My desire is to make walking with you my constant endeavor; to comply with your will, to concur with your designs and to be workers together with you. It is my desire to be dead to the world, but alive unto you; to walk as a citizen of Your Kingdom in good and bad times. I desire to be a teacher and preacher and a proclaimer of your righteousness.

Being in your presence is better than life itself. "I have

been crucified with Christ, and it is no longer I that live, but Christ living in me. That life which I now live in the flesh, I live by faith in the Son of God, who loved me, and gave himself up for me" (Galatians 2:20). Like Enoch I walk by faith and not by feelings. When I am tired from my labor and become heavy laden, by faith I come to you and you give me rest. By faith I took your yoke upon me and learned of you for you are meek and lowly, by faith I found rest for my soul. By faith I trust you and believe your yoke is easy and your burden is light (Matthew 11:28-30).

I yearn for you, aiming to please you, just like Enoch "for before his translation he had this testimony, that he pleased God." (Hebrews 11:5). Like Enoch, by faith I yield to you in full surrender. I diligently seek you Father. I run to your throne for all my needs: spiritually, emotionally and physically. There is no substitute for your provision for my life.

Father, grant unto me your guidance, your wisdom, your knowledge, your understanding, your strength, your joy, your peace, your providence, your will, your most excellent way and anything and everything I may have left out. I want receive the best that you have for me; all for your good pleasure and your glory. It is in Jesus name. Amen!

Mary J. Bryant

Changing from the Inside Out

"Rejoice always. Pray without ceasing. In everything give thanks, for this is the will of God in Christ Jesus toward you."
(1 Thessalonians 5:16-18)

ur Father, in the name of Jesus, I give you thanks. My heart is rejoicing as I meditate on you. Nothing around me has changed, but what's inside me is changing. My heart looks up with a steadfast hope. My Most High God, I hallow your name. I feel the light of Jesus, the Holy Spirit, stirring on the inside of me. I sense you enlarging my territory with hope and great expectations. I don't deserve such kindness and attention, but because of who you are, grace, mercy and your compassion just keeps on coming. I am humbled before your throne of grace, worshiping you for who you are. I cannot really explain what is happening on the inside but it is better than anything the world has to offer me. Thank you for never leaving me or forsaking me. You are forever present with me.

Father, I thank you that I don't have to fret concerning my situation. I hold fast to your word that in due season I will reap if I don't give up. I will trust in you oh Lord and do good. I thank you for your protection that I may enjoy safety. Thank You that as I delight myself in You, You will give me the desires of my heart.

Father, my soul thirsts for you God. Where am I? Am I on target with your plan for me? Am I walking in your purpose? Am I pleasing to you? How is my attitude? Do I forgive others as you have forgiven me?

Father, help me be who you have predestined me to be. Help me to walk in the way I should I walk. Help me to walk by faith and not by sight for the just shall live by faith. Let your love be

18

poured in my heart by the Holy Spirit, so that I may love others as you have commanded. I pray your blessing that I may be a blessing. All that I am, I give to you. Thank you, Father for your goodness that you have shown towards me. I pray this according to your will in Jesus name, Amen.

Lead Me in Your Righteousness

"Give ear to my words, Yahweh. Consider my meditation. Listen to the voice of my cry, my King and my God; for to you do I pray". **(Psalm 5:1-2)**

It is to you and only you I offer up my morning request. As you listen to my prayer, I wait in great expectation for your answer. I will, by your great mercy, come into your presence in reverence. I bow down toward your holy hill. Lead me in your righteousness. Be merciful to me Father, because I am faint. Heal me, for my bones are in agony. My soul is in anguish. Turn your ear to me and save me oh God. Deliver me with your unfailing love; your everlasting love. I am so tired of my groaning .All my strength is gone. I love You God. You are my rock and fortress, in whom I take refuge. You are my deliverer and stronghold. I call to you who is worthy of praise.

My God you answer me when I am in distress. You protect me from my enemies and foes. Thank you for sending help to me. I delight in you Lord. Give me the desires of my heart.

My soul moans and groans out of the depth of my inner most being. I feel as though I am traveling through the Valley of Bacca. Uncover your well, Lord, while I am on this journey as a stranger here. Give me strength to hold on and hold out for I grow weary feeling I am not making a difference. Lead me in the way I should go so that I will be pleasing in your sight. In Jesus name I pray. Amen.

Strengthen Me As I Walk by Faith and Not Feelings

"Haven't I commanded you? Be strong and courageous. Don't be afraid. Don't be dismayed, for Yahweh your God is with you wherever you go".
(Joshua 1:9)

*L*ord, I hear you commanding me to be strong and of a good courage but I have become dismayed. I don't want to give way to my emotions or how things look. I denounce anything that is not of you; every dark place, every crippling thing, every deceiving thought, every imposter that tries to come into the temple, and every spirit that comes to keep me in bondage. Lord Jesus pray that my faith does not fail me, but let me stand strong and of a good courage. Help me not be dismayed, for you are with me. You are for me so who can be against me? Lead me into a victorious life; an abundant life. I can relate to Joshua for I too feel low in my eyes; not distrustful of God, and His power and His promises, but lack of confidence in myself and my own wisdom and strength. You, God, are all-sufficient.

Forgive me. I do not want what is before me to overwhelm me. You are my strength and my redeemer. In Jesus name I pray, Amen.

I Turn to the Lover of My Soul, Jesus.

*"Look on my right, and see; for there is no one who is concerned for me. Refuge has fled from me. No one cares for my soul". **(Psalm142:4)***

Who can I go to for help? Who can I turn to too deliver me? Who can I talk to for understanding? Who can I go to for comfort and security? Who can I trust with my most precious thoughts? Who can I depend on to make everything alright?

There is no one but you Lord. All my help comes from you. No one cared for my soul but you Lord, the lover of my soul. We are good at not dealing with our own issues, but I want to deal with mine. I am in a place where I am worried about the very thing you said not to worry about. I confess this to You, Lord. Please forgive me and help me to move out of my doubt and worry. I get caught up in not knowing what to do with myself. I do not know what path to take. Should I go or should I stay? If I stay can I deal with it? If I go, what will I do; where would I go? Where am I Lord? What is your purpose for my life? Why don't I know what that purpose is? Am I not walking in it yet?

I feel as though I am about to explode. Help me in my weak hour. Help me not to faint. Let your peace overtake me. I am in complete submission to your service. I willingly place myself on your Potter's wheel. Help me to walk by faith not by sight or feelings. Oh Lord, my God; Help me! I am weak and need a healing for my mind, body and soul. Help me to trust and obey you. Lead me so that I take my mind off of me and my problems. In Jesus name I pray. Amen.

A Prayer While in Distress

"From the end of the earth, I will call to you, when my heart is overwhelmed. Lead me to the rock that is higher than I."
(Psalm 61:2)

Father, my heart is enlarged. My life seems to be fading away from me. Stress has become my best friend. Where is my faith? Is it being tested? Will I pass the test? Let me walk by faith and not by sight. Why do I cry and feel so sad and helpless when I know and believe you are my help? What must I do to get passed this stage in my life? What do I need to do to mature in my faith? I don't want my heart pain to control me. Help me to transform my mind, oh Lord. Give me the divine strength to count it all joy when trials and tribulations come against me, even when I am hurt by loved ones. Jesus, help me! I didn't go to work. I just don't feel motivated. I am stuck in this place and no one knows how much pain I am in right now. There is no one I can call to tell it to. I am so glad that you are always with me; looking out for me; you know my every thought, my heart's desire. You know my potential. When your Spirit is upon me, I am stronger. I am bolder than I've ever been. My mind is sharper than ever before. Remain upon me Holy Spirit so I may walk in faith, love, forgiveness, peace, joy, understanding, knowledge, wisdom, courage, boldness, obedient, humbleness. I long for a higher place in You Lord. I need more of You Lord and less of me. In Jesus name I pray. Amen!

Mary J. Bryant

A Follow up to the Prayer of Distress

"Then they cried to Yahweh in their trouble, and he delivered them out of their distresses" **(Psalm 107:6)**

Father, it is just so amazing how you care for me. I am at a loss for words to describe all your goodness and mercy toward me. All I can truly say is to God be the glory! It was very hard for me yesterday - extremely hard, but because I put my trust in you, I was able to keep holding on. I cried out to you. You were right by my side. I don't know what tomorrow will bring, but I am cleaving to you. I need you every step of the way. There is no decision I want to make without you. There is no where I want to go without you leading me. There is nothing I want to say without you giving me the words. My life no longer belongs to me, but I owe it to you. Use me as you have purposed. I don't ever want to think without you being Lord of my thoughts. I am weak and you are strong and mighty. You are Sovereign. Oh Lord God forever be in the midst of me. I am so ready to leave this job, Lord. I know there is more for me than this, and I pray for release through you in Jesus name. So, if it is your will for me to leave very soon, let it be done. Help me to walk in your confidence Lord. Realizing I am blessed when I go and when I come and that I am the head and not the tail. Help me remember that your blessings chase me down and overtake me and you prepare a table for me in the presence of my enemies. You anoint my head with oil and my cup runs over and I am in your overflow, Lord. You have enlarged my footsteps that I may not fall. Let me bare much fruit because I am connected to you. I abide in you and you in me. Increase my passion and desire to study Your Scriptures, so that I may know your truth by revelation of the Spirit. Let your glory rest on me that will cause others to feel drawn to me. Help me to do your will. Let your power fall on me so there will be manifestation of

24

the Holy Spirit as your word says.

I am learning that life will have its ups and downs, but because I am yours, I will still be able to praise you and know that you are God. Apostle Paul puts it in Philippians 4:11 I've learn how to be content and satisfied to the point where I am not disturbed or disquieted –in whatever state I am in.

It is my prayer that all my family members are saved and come into a personal relationship and full knowledge of Jesus Christ.

Father, I sense that you have given me revelation to write a book (2007). So I am praying for the material I will need to do this. I need you to guide my mind and my hands to accomplish this. This really makes me feel good that you would place that with me to do. I am truly humbled and honored. Thank You, Father! In the Lord's name I pray. Amen!

Burdened, Burned Out, Bewildered

He has said to me, "My grace is sufficient for you, for my power is made perfect in weakness." Most gladly therefore I will rather glory in my weaknesses, that the power of Christ may rest on me."
(2 Corinthians 12:9)

ather, I am brought down low. My heart is broken and it seems unfixable because it's been broken again and again in the same place. I am not going to tell you about the troubles that surround me; I go to bed with them, I wake up with them and can't seem to escape from them. I do want to ask you if you are pleased with me. Do you count me as being faithful? Am I submitting myself unto you? Have I kept your precepts? For no matter what the test, the trial or tribulation. I need to be able to still be pleasing to you.

Acts 24:16 "Herein I also practice always having a conscience void of offense toward God and men"

I do not want to offend you Father. It is my desire to enter into your gates with thanksgiving and your court with praise. My test may have me low in spirit and I feel as though I am being held under water, fighting to live and not die. I declare the glory of the Lord. Though my trials and tribulations press me down so hard I can't hold up my head, I can still say you are the keeper of my soul. You see me even though I don't see you. As I go through this challenging time, you are a banner over me. Nothing that the enemy is trying to use against will succeed. You are my shield and protector.

Now, Father, I want to make it perfectly clear that this is not about me and my circumstances. However, it is about you. You are the God who is very great. You are clothed with honor and majesty. You are the God who covers Himself with light as with a garment; you stretch out the heavens like a curtain. You are the God who lays the beams of your upper chambers on their waters. You are the God who makes the clouds your chariot and rides on the wings of the wind. The works of your hand are great. I will sing to you all my life; I will sing praises to you as long as I live. May my mediation be pleasing to you Lord as I rejoice in you. I may not be able to say a word and tears are streaming down my face, and my bed has become my grave, but I will still have a praise living in my belly flowing like living water. I have been given the victory because Jesus died on the cross, was buried and resurrected and ascended to heaven, back to the Father. He is seated at His right hand of God, that I may be redeemed to the Father. How can I not praise and worship you Lord; I owe my life to you. As I get ready to end this entry on this day, go with me and abide in me as I abide in you for you are the Vine and I am the branch. Remain in me so that I may bear much fruit for I can do nothing without you. In Jesus, the Lord's name I pray. Amen!

Great Expectations!

"Rejoice always. Pray without ceasing. In everything give thanks, for this is the will of God in Christ Jesus toward you."
(1 Thessalonian 5:16-18)

Father, in the name of Jesus, I give you thanks. My heart is rejoicing as I meditate on you. Nothing around me has changed, but what's inside me is changing. My heart looks up with a steadfast hope. My Most High God, I praise your name. I feel the light of Jesus, His Holy Spirit stirring on the inside of me. I feel Him enlarging my territory with hope and a great expectation in you. I don't deserve such kindness and attention, but because of who you are, your grace and mercy and compassion just keeps on coming. I am humble before your throne of grace worshipping you for who you are. I can't really explain what's happening on the inside, but it is better than anything the world has to offer me. Do not ever leave me.

Please be forever present with me. I need your guidance. I need you to bridle my tongue. I need you to keep renewing my mind. I need you to order my steps. I need you to make a way out of no way. I need you to give me boldness to speak as I ought to speak. I need you to help me see the unseen and to hear the unspoken. God I need you to be God. I need Jesus to be Lord of my life. I need the Holy Spirit to give me revelation of your truth. In Jesus name I pray. Amen.

Woman after God's Heart

"For Yahweh's eyes run back and forth throughout the whole earth, to show himself strong in the behalf of them whose heart is perfect toward him. Herein you have done foolishly; for from henceforth you shall have wars." **(2 Chronicles 16:9)**

ather, I pray that my heart is perfect toward you so that you will show yourself strong on my behalf.

There is none like you God. I just think of you and I become so overwhelmed with humbleness. I can't really describe what I feel, so I will borrow the words of the Psalmist David when he was in the wilderness of Judah.

God, you are my God. I will earnestly seek you. My soul thirsts for you. My flesh longs for you, in a dry and weary land, where there is no water. So I have seen you in the sanctuary, watching your power and your glory. Because your loving kindness is better than life, my lips shall praise you. So I will bless you while I live. I will lift up my hands in your name. My soul shall be satisfied as with the richest food. My mouth shall praise you with joyful lips, when I remember you on my bed, and think about you in the night watches. For you have been my help. I will rejoice in the shadow of your wings. My soul stays close to you. Your right hand holds me up" (Psalm 63).

Truly my soul waits upon my God. You are my salvation. You alone are my rock and my salvation. You Lord are my defense, and I shall not be greatly moved. My soul waits on you, God, for my expectation is from you. You, God are my rock, my Salvation and my defense. I shall not be moved!

In you is my salvation and my glory; the rock of my strength and my refuge. I trust you at all times. I pour out my heart before you. You have power above all power and principalities. "Also to you, Lord, belongs loving kindness, for you reward every man according to his work (Psalm 62).

Come Lord Jesus! I need you. My soul within is crying to be free. My spirit is moaning and groaning for the good works you have prepared for me. I was created as your workmanship in Christ Jesus before the foundation of the world. Come to my rescue. Place those open doors in front of me that no one can close. I pray for the wisdom and courage of the Holy Spirit. Close those doors behind me that no one can open them, and give me the power to never look back. Bring me exodus from this place if I am not to be here any longer.

I want to dwell with you. I long to be your friend with a servant's heart, doing what is pleasing in your sight for your glory. My soul longs to be in your courts. My heart is crying out to you, God. Oh God, my shield, let your eyes see me as a woman after your heart.

> "For a day in your courts is better than a thousand. I would rather be a doorkeeper in the house of my God, than to dwell in the tents of wickedness. For Yahweh is a sun and a shield. Yahweh will give grace and glory. He withholds no good thing from those who walk blamelessly." (Psalm 84)

Heavenly Father, there is no god like you. Your words are life and strength to me. You have made all nations and they will acknowledge your sovereignty. They will worship and glorify your name. You are great and do wonderful things. You are God alone! Father I want to know your way, so I will live by your truth. Teach me to fear your name. I will praise you Lord, my God, with all my heart. I will glorify your name. Thank you for your mercy towards me. They are new every day. You cover me with compassion. Your grace is abundant in my life. Help me to apply my heart unto wisdom. I pray that you will show me what you would have me to do. Father let your beauty be upon me. I need you to establish the work of my hand.

Father I praise you for your excellent gifts. Help me come before your presence with thanksgiving and make a joyful noise. You, LORD, are a great God, and a great King above all gods. I worship and bow down and kneel before you. You are my God and I belong to you. Give me the ears to hear your voice and the heart to be obedient. Clothe and robe with in righteousness and truth. I love you therefore I hate evil. Thank you for preserving my soul and delivering me out of the hand of the wicked. I will have nothing to do with evil. In Jesus name I pray, Amen.

"His Eye Is On the Sparrow"

"Are not two sparrows sold for a penny? Yet not one of them will fall to the ground outside your Father's care. And even the very hairs of your head are all numbered. So don't be afraid; you are worth more than many sparrows." (Matthew 10:29-31)`

I have been feeling pretty "bummed" lately. In fact, it has been just hard getting motivated to do much of anything but while I was getting ready for work this morning, I began to hum *His Eye Is on the Sparrow*. I thought I would do some research on the origin of the song.

From Wikipedia, the free encyclopedia, I found out that in early spring of 1905, a husband and wife was traveling in Elmira, New York. They became friends with another couple, the Doolittles. Mrs. Doolittle had been bedridden for twenty years. Her husband was an incurable cripple who had to propel himself to and from his business in a wheel chair. Despite their afflictions, they lived happy Christian lives, bringing inspiration and comfort to all who knew them. When questioned about their bright hopefulness, Mrs. Doolittle replied simply "His eye is on the sparrow, and I know He watches me. The Martins imagination was sparked and then came up with a poem with the same title and Charles Gabriel supplied the music.

So I asked myself these same questions: Why are you letting these external issues get you down? Why are you dwelling in the negative things that come to keep you down? Why are you feeling like there is no one who cares about you? Why are you letting your emotions get the best of you? Because when I meditate on Matthew 10:29-31, it helps me remember that I do walk by faith and not by sight. It helps me to renew my mind that God does care about me and knows me so well the hairs on my head are numbered.

Father, thank you, that through your tender mercies, you keep reminding me of your ever abiding presence and your everlasting love you have for me. Father, help me to live a life that honors you. Help me to get to the place where my joy is never shaken by my circumstance, for the Joy of the Lord is my strength. I love you because you first loved me. You tell me how valuable I am to you, not because of my goodness, but your goodness. I desire to walk in the authority of what I have been given: in power, love and sound mind. I desire to boldly proclaim what thus says the Lord. I want to have the mind of Christ. I want to be able to walk according to the Spirit and not the flesh (old nature). I want my soul anchored in you, Lord. You are the Vine and I am the branch. Father, I thank you once again. In Jesus name I pray, Amen.

God Alone

"Be still, and know that I am God. I will be exalted among the nations. I will be exalted in the earth." (Psalm 46:10)

ather God, You are my refuge and strength, a right now help when I am in trouble. I will not fear, no matter what may be in front of me. Even when my problems seem to press in on me without ceasing, you are still God. Therefore, I will be still, and know that you are God and God alone, no god before you nor after you; no god like you. You will be exalted among the heathen; you will be exalted in the earth.

I know you will make me to hear joy and gladness; that in my brokenness I will rejoice. Though I feel as though things will remain the same and ask when Lord when? Truly I wait on you. My salvation comes from you. I pour out my heart before you for; you are my refuge, my safe place.

Father, though my problems and my troubles seem to weigh me down, I will trust in you. Please help me to trust you even more. My mouth is filled with your praise and your honor. I will speak of your goodness and salvation all the day. And my strength comes from you, Lord.

Heavenly Father, I eagerly seek you because my soul thirsts for you. There is no substitute for you. Nothing can replace your power and glory. I mediate on who you are while lying in bed at night.

I have had a true revelation of you, God, and it makes me meditate on you all day. It makes me thirst after you. There is no other source of true satisfaction. My soul does not find rest in any other way. I have seen you and have known you in a way that I can never forget and it has determined the course of my life. Knowing you has determined my attitude, my actions, the things I choose, and the way I walk. Father, satisfy my longing soul. My days and nights are consumed with thoughts of you. I listen to hear and obey your voice. I look to see you at every turn. I wait for you to show your plans and purpose for my life and how you will use me for your praise and glory. My hope is a steadfast hope, hoping in the unseen.

Father, help me to always be prepared and ready according to your power and purpose. Don't leave me out here just longing and wanting to be used by you. Help me God! I need you. Encompass me and keep me in all my ways. Lead me in your way at all times.

I have tasted and know that you are good. I can't get enough of you. I don't want to be out here in the outer courts, but move me into the holy of holies that I can worship you.

I call upon your name, Lord! Answer me and tell me great and mighty things I don't know!
Amen! In Jesus name, Amen!

Nothing else can satisfy me after having a revelation of God

God's Mercy Does Endures Forever

*"When I consider your heavens, the work of your fingers, the
moon and the stars, which you have ordained; what is man that
you think of him? What is the son of man that you care for him?"*
(Psalm 8:3-4)

believe everything Jesus did is God's best. He,
Himself, said greater works shall you do. So yes,
that is my desire to bring glory to you Father and
your Son by the Holy Spirit. I don't want to be famous but I
want to be pleasing in your sight. I want people to see my good
works and glorify you, Father. I want to do the work that I have
been created to do. To be as one crying in the wilderness,
according to Matthew 3:2 "Repent for the Kingdom of God is at
hand", so that many souls will hear the truth and believe on the
Lord Jesus that they may be saved and become disciples. Preach
and teach growing from faith to faith - maturing in the word of
God and not staying as babes but desiring the meat of the Word.
Glory to God! Oh praise your holy name. I can hardly contain
myself. There is a fire inside of me that won't be quenched no
matter the trial, tribulation or persecution. You have put a
purpose inside of me and just like with Peter You didn't give up
on him and you won't give up on me. Just like Paul you showed
up for him and you will do the same for me. Just like Samuel
none of his prayers went unanswered and You will answer my
prayers. Just like Jesus He grew in statue and wisdom and had
favor with you and men and you said that you were well pleased
with Him so you shall be with me. I shall grow in statue
(character) and divine wisdom and in favor with you and people.
You have called me beloved and you are pleased with me.

Father, I ask this not to be elevated but that I will exalt you
in all I do and say. I want all to know that you are God and you

are with me. I want the fragrance of your anointing to be smelled by those I come in contact with. I want it to be my calling card. I don't want to go without your presence or anointing being with me. Father, preserve me for your word, your message, your truth by your authority and your power.

Thank you, Father for hearing my prayer. I believe you will answer it according to your will. In the Lord's name I pray. Amen.

House of Honor

"Your laws remain to this day, for all things serve you."
(Psalm 119:91)

Abba, Father, your word states that those who live pure lives are happy. Those who keep your rules and obey you with their whole heart are happy. I would like to believe that I am one who lives a pure life who follows your teachings and keep your rules and obey them with my whole heart. Help me Father to walk this way before you all the days of my life.

I have planted your words in my heart so I would not sin against you, Lord. Open my eyes to see the miracles and mysteries of your teachings. I am consumed with desire for your word all the time. I am sad and tired, make me strong again as you have promised. Keep me from being dishonest. Have mercy on me so that I may obey your teachings. I have chosen the way of your truth. Give me understanding that I may live by your word. Your promise gives me hope. Father, teach me wisdom and knowledge. You made me and formed me with your hands. I love your word. My hope is in your word. Don't let me be embarrassed because of my hope. Father, cover me as with a shield.

Father God, when this world is closing in on me, please help me to remember to slip away and find a quiet place to pray. When I can't pray, listen to my heart. Continue to use me to do your will. Continue to bless me that I may be a blessing to others. Keep me strong that I may help the weak. Keep me uplifted that I may have words of encouragement for others who need lifting. I pray for those who are lost and who can't find their way. I pray for those who are misjudged and misunderstood. I pray for those who don't know you intimately.

I pray for those who don't believe, but I thank you that I believe. In Jesus' name I pray, Amen.

Growing in Christ

"...by which he has granted to us his precious and exceedingly great promises; that through these you may become partakers of the divine nature, having escaped from the corruption that is in the world by lust." (2 Peter 1:4)

Oh Father, help me to add to my faith, those qualities that will magnify your Presence in me. Help me to fulfill your design for a life of moral excellence (Virtue). Help me to study your word to gain wisdom to combat falsehood (Knowledge). Help me to revere you so much that I choose godly behavior (Self-control). Help me have a hopeful attitude even in difficulties because I am confident in your character (Perseverance). Help me to honor you in every relationship in my life (Godliness). Help me to display a warm hearted affection for brothers and sisters (Brotherly kindness). Help me to sacrifice for the good of others (Love).

Help me to develop these qualities in increasing measure and incorporate them into all parts of my life. I so want to please you. I want your stamp of approval. I want to walk in the fruit of the Spirit: love, joy, peace, forbearance, kindness, goodness, faithfulness, gentleness and self-control. I want to hate what you hate and love what you love. I want to be uncompromising to your word and sincere and compassionate toward the oppressed (widows, the poor, orphans). I so want to be strong in prayer and pure in worship. Help me to seek your Kingdom. Help me to know when to encourage and when to rebuke. Help me to decrease and you increase not for my glory but that you will be glorified in every part of my life. My eyes are toward heaven and my mind is on things from heaven.

Aww...You are so awesome! Aww... To look upon your

glorious face and to worship you warm every corner of my mortal and spiritual being. No other god is like you, nowhere, before or after you. You are God eternal! You exist outside of time. You are so awesome! I even feel your glory and praise at the tip of my fingers as I write this. Your Spirit is touching me and transforming me to the original blueprint and I love it! There is no substitute for you, Holy Spirit! You have such an awesome ministry to help us. You are at the top of my list of what I have got to have. This I request and petition in the Lord's name, Amen.

Mary J. Bryant

Off With the Old and On With the New

"For the whole law is fulfilled in one word, in this: "You shall love your neighbor as yourself." (Galatians 5:14)

Heavenly Father, thank you! You are with me right now and I sense you on the inside of me doing surgery; rebuilding, tearing down, restoring, birthing all for your glory. I have made myself available for your use in any way you see fit. I need you to prepare me in the matters of the Kingdom. You keep molding me in the things of God. I am between a joyful and humble heart and a sad heart. Help me Father. What do I do with this? You are pouring so much of yourself in me. How do I share this with others? You show me things you aren't pleased with and it makes me sad. Father, have mercy on us who say we belong to you. We need you desperately. Our hearts still need to be made new. We haven't died fully to our old nature. We don't want to let go of the things of the world. But we can't serve two masters. Help us Father. I cry out from the depths of my soul. I know you are preparing me for such a work in the Kingdom all based on LOVE. You are dealing with me even now. It is my goal to practice the love you are sharing and teaching me. I won't block the Holy Spirit from pouring love in my heart. I pray that this love will allow forgiveness and not give way to ungodly treatment of others (i.e. name calling, gossiping, bitterness, backbiting, hate, etc.). It is not easy for me to sit here at work and be overtaken by the Holy Spirit, because my mind is on doing my Father's business. You are my heart's desire. I can't stop thinking about you and what you want me to do for you. Give me my "Rehoboth", the place where I can be at rest or peace to do your will.

I know I owe my life to you. You paid such a price for me. Only you could have paid that price for redemption. I give

42

myself to you to be used for your glory. Help me surrender whatever I have not surrendered to you yet. You know what is best. You are God and Creator. You are just and know what is right. You are the way and know the way I should take. Oh my heart is so full of your Spirit. My mind is clear, my words flow like a river. My God, you do this to me and for me. Thank You! You take this earthen vessel called Mary and pour your wonderful treasure in me, to make me into an invaluable servant for your Kingdom. I serve you on purpose and willingly. I choose to serve you this day forward - put it in your book.

Jesus! I love YOU! There is no one like you Father. I love you because you first loved me. Everywhere I turn you are there. You are in my thoughts even now. Everything I hear and see reminds me that you are right here seeing and hearing it also. I believe you to be God who created the world and everything in it. I believe you are God the Father, God the Son, and God the Holy Spirit. I believe by the faith that Jesus has started in me and He keeps perfecting it. I don't need to know how you are three persons in one. Because you are, God, and I don't need to have an explanation for everything, just faith to believe and receive. Do I have questions? Yes, but I don't have to have an answer because I trust you, God.

You are God and I believe you are who you say you are, AMEN!

Mary J. Bryant

Praying for Revelation Knowledge

"...that the God of our Lord Jesus Christ, the Father of glory, may give to you a spirit of wisdom and revelation in the knowledge of him" (Ephesians 1:17)

Today is a peculiar day. It is as though I am in a bubble, and although people are near I feel so far away from them. The atmosphere is even different. I hear people talking who are right beside me, yet their voices sound distant. I am not sure how else to explain it. I am just trying to be still and know that God is God, and LORD of my life.

Father, speak to me God, make my ears to hear your voice telling me which way to go or what to say or do. Help me open up my soul and my spirit to hear, receive and obey what you speak. I plead with you to look upon me as your servant who is thirsty and hungry for you. I seek your face. Give me ears to hear you; eyes to see you; a heart to receive you and the spirit to obey and grace to trust you. Your way is perfect. You are a just God who will always be holy. There is nothing I want and need more than I need you. Let me remain as the apple of your eyes, pleasing to you in every way and a sweet fragrance to your nose. Don't know what I would do without you and I don't want to find out. Never take Your Holy Spirit from me. Help me to find my place in you and grow in the knowledge of Jesus Christ, His wisdom and spiritual understanding. I want to live a life worthy of the Lord. I want to be pleasing and fruitful in every good work. Father, strengthen me with all might, according to your glorious power. I pray that I have patience and longsuffering with joyfulness, giving thanks unto the Father.

Father, make me a servant, according to the gift of the grace of God by the effectual working of your power.

Oh Lord God, I praise you! O how excellent is your name in all the earth! Your glory is above the heavens. The heavens declare your glory and the firmament show your handy work. Your word is perfect, converting the soul. Your word is right, rejoicing the heart. Lord, your commandments are pure, enlightening the eyes. To fear you is clean, enduring forever. Your judgments are true and righteous.

Father, lead me in your truth and teach me, for you are my salvation. Please keep me from presumptuous sins so that they will not have dominion over me. Keep me upright and innocent from great transgression.

Yes, Lord, Yes! In Jesus name, Amen!

I Decrease So That He Can Increase

"Praise Yahweh, my soul, and don't forget all his benefits"
(Psalm 103:2)

Father, you are He who forgives me of my sins and heals all my diseases. You save my life from the grave and provide me with love and mercy. You satisfy me with good things and make me young again, like the eagle. I dare not take any god before you, because there is none like you, anywhere! Glory and honor are in your presence. Strength and gladness are in your place. As you reveal yourself to me more and more, help me to be obedient to your command, and respond according to your will. I praise and honor your holy name in all I do and all I say. You have paid a great price for my redemption and I don't take it for granted, the value of your precious priceless blood that was shed for me. You have proven yourself faithful and I want to prove myself faithful as well. You have shown yourself merciful and forgiving and I, too, want to follow in your steps. You have shown your great compassion towards me and I too want to show compassion. I need my life to reflect who you are in me. I want your very best. So I offer myself to you for your use and your pleasure.

You are growing inside me. There is a stretching and expanding inside me, Father. I don't know how or when you will use me, but I want to be ready and have a "Yes" on my lips, when you call. I feel a great work that is going on in the inside of me. Nothing I do satisfies me. I go through my day desiring and craving to do a greater work for you, Lord.

Oh Father, I sit and wait patiently for you. I go about my day in faith, looking and waiting for you and to move mightily on my behalf. I want to wear your seal of approval like I wear a garment. I want everyone to know that I am your beloved daughter and that you are well pleased with me. I want what I do and say to always honor you and glorify you. I know I need your Spirit to enable me to do these things. I am available to you, submitted and yielded. It is Your Holy Spirit that will provide me with power to do these things and all you have called me to do. In Jesus name I pray, Amen.

Pressing My Way through It All

"Cast your burden on Yahweh, and he will sustain you. He will never allow the righteous to be moved." (Psalm 55:22)

I am coming to cast my cares on you, Father. I am burdened with the cares of this life, including the heartbreak, heartache and pain, disappointments and frustrations. They have overwhelmed my soul and weakened my spirit. So now I turn to you the keeper and sustainer of my life. Let me enter into your place of rest. Deliver my soul and spirit up to your holy presence. Forgive me as I forgive those who have hurt me in my heart and seem not to care. If I have not forgiven anyone, please show me because I want to be a forgiver without question. I want to live my life trying and doing what is right before you and people. Cause me not to give or take offense but help me to discipline myself by mortifying my body, deadening my carnal affections, bodily appetites, and worldly desires. Help me have a clear, unshaken and blameless, conscience, void of offense, toward you and people.

You have brought me this far on my journey and I don't want to turn around now. My goal is to be hidden in you, Jesus. I don't want to stop or turn around. I want to continue on my path for you Lord. I don't want this burden to disqualify me before your eyes Father. I still want to be "eis emeen eudioua", a sweet savor to your nostril. I want to be well-pleasing in your sight.

I have gotten off track; my carnal affections have taken some of my attention. Hide me in your secret place; revive me again for your service; build and restore me for your glory. I am coming to you with my cares and my burdens, believing that when no one else cares, you care about me. Father, lead me way back to your throne of grace. Fill me with the power of your love once again that I can conquer all things in Jesus name. Bring the light back to my eyes because my eyes are the candle of the Lord.

Thank you, Father, that you are not far from me and that you hear my cry and see my tears. You are close to me because I am brokenhearted. Give me hind's feet to climb this mountain that is before me, knowing that no mountain is impossible to climb with you on my side. All things are possible with God.

Help me think on those things that are pure, lovely, praise worthy, and excellent. Hear my heart's cry oh LORD! I continue to press my way. Do a mighty work in me for my good and for your glory. Let the oil of your anointing cover me.

I close my eyes and lay my head on my opened hands. I am weakened by the cares of my life; help me to magnify YOU, Father, so my problems won't seem bigger than you. Help me to endure in my trials. Help me to pass the test, when I am tested. Help me to grow and prosper in Jesus Christ.

In the midst of my challenges, I believe you make all things work together for my good. It is your purpose to build endurance in me. I endure these challenges as they go from one degree to the next. I am back in focus in realizing you are still at work building my character. I renew my mind that your grace will see me through. Your grace is sufficient and in my weakness your strength is made perfect. I thank you for your grace Father.

Thank you for hearing and answering my prayer. It is in Jesus' name I pray, Amen.

Resting in His Absolute Goodness

*"Ascribe to Yahweh the glory due to his name.
Worship Yahweh in holy array"* **(Psalm 29:2)**

*"One thing I have asked of Yahweh, that I will seek after, that I
may dwell in Yahweh's house all the days of my life, to see
Yahweh's beauty, and to inquire in his temple."* **(Psalm 27:4)**

Father, thank you, and I praise you! I worship you in the beauty of holiness. All true beauty reflects some of who you are (I Am). I believe You, Father, are working your ways in me. You are the divine artist creating loveliness within my very being. Clean out all the clutter to make room for the Holy Spirit to take full residence of my heart. You are like a purifying fire and like laundry soap. I submit to your refining fire. I let go of everything you choose to take away. You know how I am created and what I am created for.

I confess my sense of security does not rest in what I have, my job or anything or anyone. I depend on you. Your presence provides me with total fulfillment. I understand that I have to be satisfied with much or with little, accepting either as your will for the moment. I don't want to be grasping and controlling but learning to release and receive. Help me to cultivate this receptive stance by trusting you in every situation at all times.

Abba, Father! How I love you. How I love your Word. It purifies my very soul. I am transformed into your likeness and image, Praise God! Teach me to fear your name, for you are Sovereign and holy. In the Lord's name I do pray. AMEN!

oems

These Poems capture the very essence of my relationship with Jesus by the inspiration of the precious Holy Spirit. When we know "we are wonderfully and fearfully made" (Psalm 139:14) in the "image and likeness of God" (Genesis 1:26), there is a change that takes place in the new heart after being born-again. The heart begins to hunger and thirst after more of Jesus.

> *"I have loved you, my people, with an everlasting love! With unfailing love, I have drawn you to myself!" Jeremiah 31:3*

Fully God, Fully Man

(Complete in Jesus)

By Mary J. Bryant
7/16/10

Fully God, fully man
Since before time began
God the Father, the Creator had a plan.

Fully God, fully man
He was Emanuel,
God with us.

Fully God, fully man
He gave up His home in glory
So that we might have the victory

Fully God, fully man
He preached the Good news
With His Word, we never loose.

Fully God, fully man
He healed the sick,
Blinded eyes could see,
Lame legs could walk,
Deaf ears could hear,
Unclean flesh was made clean,
He did all this without magic or tricks
He even made demons flee.

Fully God, fully man
He took all our sins to the cross
That no one would be lost.
Only He could pay the cost
Of a debt He did not owe.
But on the cross He was made low.

Fully God, fully man
On the cross He shed His blood.
What a great show of His love.
For on that tree He gave His only Son
And if we believe,
 New life is begun.

Fully God, fully man
Buried in a borrowed tomb.
But death had no room.
For on that third day,
He came back from the dead,
Resurrected with all power;
Now He sits as the head.

Fully God, fully man
It is in Jesus we are made full in Him.
It is in Jesus we are complete.
And have everything we need.
Jesus, fully God, fully man

You

Confession to the Lord
By Mary J. Bryant
(2/6/09)

You keep me company when I am lonely.

You are my joy when I am sad.

You mend my heart when it has been broken.

You are my healing when I am sick.

You are my peace when I am troubled.

You are my light when I am in darkness.

You love me when I am not loved.

You wipe my tears away when I cry.

You are my comforter when I need comforting.

You make me whole when I am broken.

You fill me up when I am empty.

You are my friend when I am friendless.

You hold me when I need holding.

You protect me when I am in danger (seen and unseen).

You sought me and found me when I was lost.

You show me the way when I lose my way.

You guide me when I am confused.

You are my strength when I am weak.

You energize me when I am weary.

You restore me when I am burnt out.

You carry me when I can't carry myself.

You give me the words to say when I don't know what to say.

You teach me how to pray when I don't know what to pray.

You are my help when I am in trouble.

You lift me up when I am down.

You give me hope when I am in despair.

You are my stronghold when the enemy tries to get a foothold.

You provide for me when I am in need.

You give me water when I am thirsty.

You give me bread when I am hungry.

You are my rock when I am on sinking sand.

You give me rest when I labor and am heavy burdened.

You give me *your* light yoke when my yoke is heavy.

You give me forgiveness when I sin against *You.*

Mary J. Bryant

You came to save me when I was lost in all my sins.

You became my Savior when I needed salvation.

You paid the price when I couldn't pay my debt.

You, nobody but *You Lord!!!*

Alone with My Jesus

Mary J. Bryant
February 2, 2012

Alone with my Jesus
Through Him alone frees us
from the darkness of death
and gives us our Father's breath,
the breath that gives us life.
Life that is renewed and reborn,
Reborn - no more to be alone.
But to rest upon His promise,
the promise of eternity.
So we can worship Him in that New City.
He is the beginning and the end.
There we will be in His presence,
As He sits on the throne.
Alone with my Jesus
Oh come and see
My LORD and Savior and me.

Mary J. Bryant

In My Quiet Place

Mary J. Bryant
April 24, 2012

In my quiet place,
I am not alone.
In my quiet place,
All fear and stress are gone.
In my quiet place,
Time stands still-neither here nor there.
In my quiet place,
I am restored and renewed.
In my quiet place,
Oh my sweet quiet place
sent from above;
Where I rest in my Father's love.
In my quiet place,
no one else can give such care and tenderness.
In my quiet place,
can't really describe this place;
words aren't adequate enough.
In my quiet place,
I am so grateful to be here, just me,
God the Father, God the Son, God the Holy Spirit-
the blessed TRINITY!

Just Jesus!

Mary J. Bryant

The first born
From the dead,
Who after He died
The veil was torn.
Who not one word of Him was said,
Death could not hold Him when it tried.

Just Jesus!

The Way, the Truth, and the Life,
Whose peace can keep you through pain and strife.
The Good Shepherd who know me by name.
Who is never changing, always the same,
The Lamb Who takes away the sin of the world.
Who does not care if you are a boy or a girl.

Just Jesus!

The One John baptized in the Jordan.
Who came to save us because of God's love,
The One Who when He came up from the water,
There came from Heaven a dove,
That remained on Him in the wilderness.
To pass the tempting of the evil one's test.

Mary J. Bryant

Just Jesus!

The Great I Am, the Amen.
Who is the faithful, tried and true,
The One Who can redeem men again.
He who gave His life for you and me,
Who causes old things to become new,
In the end we will eat from the tree [of life].

Just Jesus!

The lily of the valley, bright and morning star,
Who is the resurrection,
He is the best by far.
Through Him there comes a new creation.
Better than silver and gold;
By His blood we are made whole.
Better than diamonds and pearls;
It is He Who created the world.

Just Jesus!

My Heart's Desire

Mary J. Bryant
March 12, 2009

He first loved me and now I can love Him too.
Because I was lost and didn't know what to do.
He saw me being formed inside my mother,
He knows all my faults and weakness,
Still He cares for me and loves me like no other.

My heart's desire

He loves me so…
I never knew love could be so sweet.
In His love I grow and grow.
He who is my Shepherd and my King
In my darkest valley, He is my everything!

My heart's desire

In Him I delight myself greatly.
His love is oh so faithful and true!
Now that I have found Him,
I'll stick to Him like glue.
Who don't love the Lord?
He can be everything to them.
Just accept Him and believe His Word.
Come to Him NOW…for He will show you the way.
Choose Him Now… Choose Him today.

For He will show you what to do
Come as you are.
Forget about the "old" and walk in the "new".
His way is the best way by far.

My heart's desire

Above Him there is no other.
When I think of Him my heart does flutter.
With every beat, I thirst for Him even more;
Please don't ever leave me alone-
But continue to pour, pour; pour
For I hasten to your throne

My heart's desire

He is waiting for you;
Come to Him while you can be saved.
Make Him your heart's desire.
What will you do?
Don't let time expire;
For you and me His life He gave,
So that we might be saved.
…The Lord… *My Heart's Desire*

My Soul Yearns...

Mary J. Bryant
February 2, 2012

Oh my soul yearns to be at rest
In the presence of my LORD and my God.
Is it because I am put to yet another test.
Yearning to be my Father's best.
As I walk this narrow way my comfort is in His staff and rod
Oh my soul yearns to be set free.
Free so I can be who God's call me to be.
To be Mary, my authentic self,
And not just another clone sitting on a shelf.
Oh my soul yearns to soar
Far above what my eyes can see.
Never to turn back, but always reaching for more.
Going and growing from the temporary.
Oh my soul yearns to be in union with
He who created me.
Where my Father and I are as one again,
Depending totally on the Trinity.
Oh my soul yearns to commune with Him,
To have His Holy Spirit to change me from within.
To be so pressed by Him, it's no longer I that lives
But Jesus Christ who forgives.
Take my soul, my will, my mind
Oh Father God make me thine.
Take hold of my soul and make me whole
Show me your mysteries of things not told

Oh my soul yearns for you.

To be all yours is what I dream.

To be all yours; tried and true.

Only You LORD reign supreme

Take hold of my soul it yearns for  *You!*

Oh How Sweet

Mary J. Bryant
November 26, 2008

Oh how sweet to call on the name of Jesus.
That name that is above all names.
That name that remains forever the same.

Oh how sweet to call on the name of Jesus.
At that name every knee shall bow and every tongue shall confess.
In that name there is holy blessedness.

Oh how sweet to call on the name of Jesus.
That name that is the first and the last.
That name nothing or no one can surpass.

Oh how sweet to call on the name of Jesus
That name that is the Lord of host.
That name that came to save the lost.

Oh how sweet to call on the name of Jesus.
That name that gives peace during our test.
That name that all who are burdened and heavy laden can find rest.

Oh how sweet to call on the name of Jesus.
That name that is Lord of lords and King of kings.
That name that reigns over everyone and everything.

Oh how sweet to call on the name of Jesus.
That name that is sweeter than honey.
That name that is worth more than money.

Oh how sweet to call on the name of Jesus!

Through His Eyes

Mary J. Bryant (5/20/10)

In the beginning, He looked at what He created thus far and said that it was good. Then He created me from within and said it was very good. See I was created from the very essence of God. I was created from the heart of God. So how can I not see myself through His eyes? The Father who created my innermost being is the one who knitted me together in my mother's womb - even before the foundation of the earth. My frame was not hidden from Him, but His eyes saw my unformed body. Through His eyes I am fearfully and wonderfully made.

How can I not see myself through His eyes when He has created me in Christ Jesus for good works even before time began? His grace was poured out on me abundantly along with the faith and love in Christ Jesus. Through His eyes I am accepted in the Beloved.

How can I not see myself through His eyes when He, the Mighty One, rejoices over me with gladness? He quiets me with His love. He rejoices over me with singing. Through His eyes, I'm the apple of His eyes; how can I not see myself through His eyes when He sent His Son, Jesus, to be my exchange on that cross. He allowed Himself to be punished so that I would be forgiven. He allowed Himself to be wounded so that I am healed. He became sin with my sinfulness so that I would be made righteous with His righteousness. He died my death so that I would receive His life. He was made a curse so that I would enter into His blessing. He endured my poverty so that I would share His abundance. He bore my shame so that I would share His glory. He endured my rejection so that I would be accepted with the Father. He was cut off by death so that I would be joined to God forever. How can I not see myself through His eyes?

Alas, through His eyes, He sees me clothed with the garments of salvation and covered with the robe of righteousness. And He has prepared a place for me to worship Him forever.

Who am I not to see myself through His eyes? Through His eyes, I will see myself – no longer defined by my environment, my disappointments, my hurt and pain, and no one or no thing that tries to steal my identity in Christ.

Through God's eyes, I am accepted in the Beloved, called, chosen and faithful.

Mary J. Bryant

Recious Moments

recious Moments are just that. I have been journaling since my teenage years, and as my relationship grew with the Lord, my journaling subject matters changed. The very heart of the pages that contain my most intimate thoughts, desires, disappoints, heartaches, etc., took on a whole new design. For this time I had my Jesus with me and I could just open up to Him, knowing He was there with me.

In 2001, my life took a turn downward, but in looking back, it was just what I needed to go through to really begin to search for my place in Christ. David wrote, "It was good that I was afflicted so that I might learn your decrees." (Psalm119:71 NIV 1984) In the midst of all the suffering, I was led to secure the salvation of my soul. I learned to not only seek God but to obey Him. Therefore, no matter the suffering, I knew it couldn't compare to the journey I was going on with the Lord. Apostle Paul puts it like this in Roman 8:18, "The sufferings we have now are nothing compared to the great glory that will be shown to us."

In my seeking, searching and yearning, I sought the promised Holy Spirit.

Just reading God's words, encouraged me not to give up but to continue to seek Him. I just thank Him for being such a wise and all-knowing God with all power in His hands. He is Alpha and Omega yet He is a present God, my strength, my being, my breath. God is my all in all. I don't want to go without God leading me and guiding me through life. I can't make it without Him. I don't know about anyone else, but I might as well drop dead right now if God withdrew Himself from me.

So I hope these Precious Moments encourage you and move you to grow in the Lord. Who knows maybe you will start to have your own "precious moments" with the Father. Be Blessed.

You Are Worthy Lord

He has on his garment and on his thigh a name written, "KING OF KINGS, AND LORD OF LORDS." (Revelation 19:16)

*L*ord, it is all about you and your praise. Take me out of myself and put more of you in me. Thank you for teaching me how to live by your Word. Show me how to love those who hurt me and also my enemies. Cause me to meditate on your words and not on my problems.

When my heart is troubled and my mind is filled with turmoil, you hide me in your secret tabernacle under the shadow of your wings, so I may have that peace that passes all understanding. You help me to grow in grace so that those around me may get a glimpse of your glory. So you alone will get the praise. You break every yoke in my life that has me imprisoned within myself. You cause my faith to increase that I may be able to move mountains out of my way.

You bless me exceedingly abundantly above that which I can ever hope or ask of you. Teach me to do your will. Allow me to see Mary through your eyes. Let me reach the potential you have purposed for me. Let me not fear life or what it may bring my way, but help me to lean and depend on you, everlasting Father. (Ephesians 3:20)

I don't always know what to pray for Father, so teach me how to pray and what to pray for. Open my mouth with holy boldness that I may praise you and worship you no matter who is looking. Don't let me be ashamed to shout Hallelujah to your name, because you alone deserve the highest praise.

Wonderful Jesus!

*"Yahweh, our Lord, how majestic is your name in all the
earth, who has set your glory above the heavens!"*
(Psalm 8:1)

h Lord how excellent is your name. You are great and
awesome. I tremble at your presence with such humility
and confession that you are God, the creator of heaven
and the earth.

Thank you for supplying my every need. I get so
overwhelmed when you feed me manna from on high; when you
provide me with such divine substance that makes me hungrier
and thirstier for you. I just ask that you help me to put all these
things into perspective and commit them to my memory.

I want all of you, not just a portion, but the fullness of God,
nothing mixing with your truth. Just the plain old untouched,
unchanged, undiluted, saving, freeing truth. I don't want to live
with or settle for any other gospel or any other way because
Jesus is the truth, the life, and the way. Equip me for service in
Your Kingdom.

I'm sitting here trying to contain myself, but your glory and
your goodness makes me want to shout! Thank you for being my
Lord, and thank you for first loving me. Thank you for knocking
at the door to my heart and giving me an ear to hear your voice.
Thank you for coming in and supping with me and me with you.

I can't ask for anything more because in you there is fullness
of joy. I once again confess you to be Lord of my life. I once
again submit myself to you, yielding and willing in obedience to
you, believing you will enable me for whatever assignment you
have for me. Though I may faultier at times, I always end up at
your feet because you love me with an everlasting love. I sigh
not because I am bored but because I am so in love with you and
my heart feels so content right now. I am at peace and I thank
you. You are indeed my refuge. Show me the way I should go.
Everything that I am and ever hope to be is in Jesus, my Savior,
my Lord, and my Redeemer, Amen!

Mary J. Bryant

The Lord Has Done Great Things

"Let all that I am praise the LORD; may I never forget the good things he does for me." (Psalm 103:1 NLT)

This is the song I got out of the shower singing this morning because my soul does bless you, LORD. You think of me and care for me. You made me a little lower than the heavenly beings and crowned me with glory and honor. LORD, God how majestic is your name. I will praise you with all my heart, I will tell of all your wonders. I will be glad and rejoice in you. I will sing praise to your name O Most High God.

I trust you LORD. Father I have heard the Gospel and I believe, by faith in Jesus, your Son, who you sent into the world, that He may glorify you. Everyone who believe and repent and turn to you will be saved. I trust you in the good times and the bad times; when I'm happy and when I'm sad. I have put all my trust in you. You are my hope. I know you will never leave me or forsake me. I don't mind waiting because I know you will make everything alright. In fact, you have made everything alright.

You are waiting with outstretched arms to welcome whosoever will come into your Kingdom. You are the Truth, the Life, and the Way. There is no other way in which we can be saved.

I just love you LORD. You overwhelm me with your presence. I am in awe of you. I reverence your holy name. Every time I read or hear about you my heart skips a beat and I want to be like Mary and sit at your feet and worship you. I want to eat of you and know of you and learn of you. I want your word to saturate me, that I may have knowledge and understanding. I don't want to let this moment go, I am consumed with you; yet I am not full or tired, but I yearn for more, I thirst for you. I hunger for more. I feel like Peter when he said in the John 6:68, "Lord, to whom shall I go? You have the words to eternal life." I know and believe that you are God." Nothing or no one can compare to you. There is no substitute for you. There was none before you and there is none after you. You are God alone! Amen, Glory to God!

Father, I know I will be tested, but I pray for your grace and mercy to abound towards me so that I will pass every test. I know I will go through trials and tribulations, but I pray for your sustaining and keeping power. I pray for your compassion that never fails, so that I will have the right attitude and response to my trials, that I may display godly character for your glory. Help me to walk in humility by knowing who I am in you. Let me walk boldly in your purpose for me and help me to keep my eyes fixed on Jesus. Help me discern between what is right and wrong; good and evil, so I may have the power to hate, what you hate and love what you love.

My Daily Bread

*"Give us today our daily bread." **(Matthew 6:11)***

Dear Lord,

I sat here the entire day with you on my mind. I hunger and thirst after righteous. I am in awe of your power. I am in reverence of your sovereignty. Oh LORD, what would you have me to do? What would you have me to say? Where would you have me go?

Here I am, ready and willing to do your will, O my God. Your law is in my heart. Help me proclaim the good news of righteousness. Help me not restrain my lips. Help me declare your faithfulness and your salvation. Help me not to conceal your loving kindness and your truth.

What would you have me do? Here I am; I am your servant willing to do your will. You have made me fearfully and wonderfully. You know the plans you have for me, and the good work you've started in me, you will finish. All of my hopes and dreams are embedded in you. I don't want just a job unless it is the job you want me to have. I don't want to make any decisions without you being right there in the midst of it. I want and desire to be obedient to You, O, Lord. I pant for you like the deer pants for water. Your wisdom I desire oh Lord. As I write I am so overwhelmed with You, God. I feel engulfed by your presence. I just want to stay right here worshiping at your throne.

Overwhelmed in His Presence

"My soul longs, and even faints for the courts of Yahweh. My heart and my flesh cry out for the living God". (Psalm 84:2)

s I was sitting at my kitchen table this morning before coming to work, I was listening to the song "Blessed Assurance". Tears started to flow from my eyes as I felt humility grow in my heart surrendering to Christ. I acknowledge His presence by reverencing His sovereignty and holiness. I could have stayed right there worshiping Him. It just felt right and proper. I hated to break that moment to leave for work. Nobody but the Lord!

Frances J Crosby wrote the famous hymn Blessed Assurance:

Blessed assurance Jesus is mine! Oh, what a foretaste of glory divine! Heir of salvation, purchase of God, born of His Spirit, washed in His blood. This is my story, this is my song, praising my Savior all the day long; this is my story; this is my song, praising my Savior all the day long. Perfect submission, perfect delight, visions of rapture now burst on my sight; Angles, descending, bring from above echoes of mercy, whispers of love. Perfect submission, all is at rest, I in my Savior am happy and blest, watching and waiting, looking above, filled with His goodness, lost in His love.

Mary J. Bryant

More of Jesus and Less of Me

*"For to us a child is born. To us a son is given; and the
government will be on his shoulders. His name will be called
Wonderful, Counselor, Mighty God, Everlasting Father, Prince
of Peace." (Isaiah 9:6)*

h how my heart yearns for more of you, Jesus. There is nothing that can take the place of my thirst and hunger for you. You have drawn me to your throne and still drawing me. I feel faint from your love. I am overwhelmed by your holy presence. I stand in a reverent awe of your sovereignty. You fill me with your Spirit until I'm running over, yet I still thirst and hunger for your righteousness. How do I share this passion to everyone else? I want to share you, Jesus, with all I meet. I want everyone to know you for themselves. I want to share your love with everyone who wants this unconditional love. I want others to experience your amazing grace and mercy that is new every morning. I want people to experience your compassion that never fails, this consuming fire. You are the only Way, the only Truth and the only Life. You are our reconciler. Romans 5:11 states "We also rejoice in God through our Lord Jesus Christ, through whom we have now received the reconciliation." Praise God. I love you so.

"And the Spirit of the LORD will rest on him the Spirit of wisdom and understanding, the Spirit of counsel and might, the Spirit of knowledge and the fear of the LORD. He will delight in obeying the LORD. He will not judge by appearance nor make a decision based on hearsay. He will give justice to the poor and make fair decisions for the exploited. The earth will shake at the force of his word, and one breath from his mouth will destroy the wicked. He will wear righteousness like a belt and truth like an undergarment. You are so faithful. You are the first and the last. There is no God beside you. Thank You for first loving me, Lord God. Not only do I have the victory, but in you I triumph. Praise your holy name. I bow down in reverence to you. I surrender my life to you. My wants, desires, plans or goal is nothing compared

76

to your plans. My will is surrendered to your will. I freely am a bond-servant to you, seeking to do your will. Help me to be bold in all that you would have me to do, with love. Help me to hear your voice and be obedient." (Isaiah 11:2-5 NLT)

Mary J. Bryant

I Love Him Because He First Love Me

*"This is real love – not that we loved God, but that he loved us
and sent his Son as a sacrifice to take away our sins."*
(1 John 4:10 NLT)

h how sweet to know Jesus. I hear His name and I just become so engulfed with humbleness and gratitude to how He came to reconcile us back to the Father. And I go into worship because of who He is. Isaiah calls Him Wonderful Counselor, Mighty God, Everlasting Father, Prince of Peace. His Presence is what I long for. I long to know what is the hope of His calling, what are the riches of the glory of His inheritance in the saints and what is the exceeding greatness of His power toward us who believe, according to the working of His mighty power which He worked in Christ when He raised Him from the dead and seated Him at His right hand in the Heavenly places, far above all principality and power and might and dominion, and every name that is named, not only in this age but also in that which is to come (Ephesians 1:18-21)

Oh how I love Him so because He first loved me. I need Him not only in my life but I need Him to be the head of my life. I can't do without Him. I'm so glad He came to save me. I know He lives and He lives in my heart. Oh how my mind is stayed on Jesus; my hope, my joy, my peace, my wonderful counselor, my everlasting father, my all in all. Oh bless His holy name. To be more like Jesus is what I desire.

Jesus, More than Enough

"Yahweh is my shepherd: I shall lack nothing."
(Psalm 23:1)

*J*esus, you are my life because you came from heaven to earth to save me. You went to that cross carrying all my sins, curses, sickness, and diseases with you. I gladly and willingly give my life to you. Every part of me belongs to you. Come and abide in me and I abide in you until we are one—until I'm decreased and you are increased. You knew me before I was formed in my mother's womb. You know the way I should take and I want to walk in your way. Just let me sit at your feet because I am hungry for you. I hunger to come to the full knowledge and understanding of you. I am hungry for your truth and your way. But I just don't want all this for myself but for all who are hungry for you.

Lord God, you mean so much to me. You are everything to me.

When I was lonely, you kept me company.
When I was sad; you were my joy.
When I was brokenhearted; you mended my heart.
When I was sick; you healed me.
When I was troubled; you were my peace.
When I was in darkness; you were my light.

When I hated, you loved me.
When I cried, you wiped my tears away.
When I needed comforting; you comforted me.
When I was broken; you made me whole.
When I was friendless; you were my friend.
When I needed to be held; you held me in your arms.

When in danger (seen and unseen) you protected me.
When I was lost, you sought me and found me.
When I was confused, you guided me.
When I was weak, you were my strength.
When I was weary; you energized me.
When I was burned out; you restored me.

When I couldn't carry myself; you carried me.
When I didn't know what to say; you gave me the words to say.
When I was down; you lifted me up.
When I was in despair; you gave me hope.
When I was lost in all my sins; you came and saved me.

Times of Refreshing

*"He restores my soul. He guides me along the right paths for his name's sake." **(Psalm 23:3)***

ord God, you overwhelm me with your power, your greatness, your awesomeness, your majesty, and your faithfulness. You are the Most High God and I humble myself under your mighty hand. I submit myself to you. Oh Lord God, how I delight myself in you. You console and comfort me right where I am. My eyes are fixed on you. My ears are inclined unto you. You are just a wonder in my soul. You are like fire shut-up in my bones. Who do I tell about your goodness? How do I tell about your goodness? How do I tell about your love? My heart is bursting open with love for you because your love has been poured out in my heart by the Holy Spirit. Help me to put on that love and walk in that love so others can see you in me and glorify you. I pant for you like the deer pant for water. I thirst for you in a dry place. I hunger for you – give me this daily bread for I do not live by bread alone but by every word that comes forth out your mouth. Thank You.

Every time I'm in Your Presence my soul gets refreshed and I can go on from glory to glory.

Isaiah 40:11 "as a shepherd carries a lamb, I have carried you close to my heart."

TIMES OF REFRESHING

COME INTO MY GARDEN,
REST AWHILE WITH ME.
ENJOY THE FRAGRANT ESSENCE
OF FELLOWSHIP SO SWEET.
TAKE TIME TO RELAX IN
THE JOY OF MY EMBRACE.
COME APART AND SAVOR
FATHOMLESS PEACE AND GRACE.
I CAME INTO HIS GARDEN
IT WAS SO PEACEFUL THERE.
THE FRAGRANCE OF HIS PRESENCE
DISPELLED MY EVERY CARE.
AND AS I RESTED THERE WITH HIM

GERTRUDE JEFFERIES

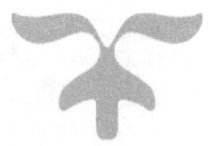

Alone with You

*"Yahweh, your God, is among you, a mighty one who will save. He will rejoice over you with joy. He will calm you in his love. He will rejoice over you with singing." **(Zephaniah 3:17)***

*"Great is the LORD! He is most worthy of praise! He is to be feared above all gods. The gods of other nations are mere idols, but the LORD made the heavens! Honor and majesty surround him; strength and beauty fill his sanctuary." **(Psalm 96 NLT)***

*Y*ou came and visited with me this morning as I drove in to work like you have done so many times before. Oh how I thirst and hunger to be called into your presence as your daughter, even when I am feeling depressed, you never turn your back on me. You never give up on me. You never let me fall. You draw me to your bosom and just feed me with your manna. I am so humbled by your holy presence. My heart rejoices and is grateful for your love toward me. You have begun a good work in me and you are preparing me for your service. I am like Samuel when you call I will answer "Speak, for your servant hears". I will be like Mary and say, "Behold the maidservant of the Lord! Let it be to me according to your word." For you know the plans you have for me, plans of good and not evil and you will perfect it until the coming of Jesus Christ. I bless you, Oh Lord. I yearn to dwell in your Holy place, to go into the Holy of Holies, and to sing praises to you and worship at your feet. My passion burns for you. Teach me your way and lead me into your path forever. Teach me your word, give me understanding so I will be enlightened and stand on your truth always. Give me your Holy Spirit so I will not only be a hearer but also a doer of your word and others will see the God in me and desire a relationship with you.

I sit here at my desk with no other agenda or plan but to hear your voice and obey it. I sit here waiting for you to move in my life to move any way you so choose. I give you free course in my life and over my life. I do this willingly and happily without hesitation or reservation. You have created me. You shaped and formed me in my mother's womb. You know me by name and you know me inside out. Let my will be lost in your will. I feel so safe in your presence, so protected. You give me peace that passes all understanding. I'm so very grateful to you Father God. I trust you with all that I am and everything that I have. I trust you with my family. Bind us together with your unfailing love, your faithfulness, your compassion, your forgiveness, your mercy and grace.

Lord, you are so precious to me. You loved me long before I loved you. Your eyes were on me long before my eyes were on you. You drew me to you and I was given favor to receive you. Thank You! I am so grateful, honored and humbled. I bow down my ear to you. I thank you that when I am poor and needy, you hear me. I have given you my soul. Preserve it for you have made it holy. Thank you for saving me because I put my trust in you. Thank you for being so merciful unto me, Father. I cry to you daily. Thank you that you are good and ready to forgive. Thank you for being so merciful to all who call on your holy and righteous name. You listen to my prayer and have compassion on my supplications. In my days of trouble I call on you and you answer me. Thank you. There is no god like you. There is no god who can even compare to you.

No other god does the wondrous works that you do. It is awesome and mighty in our sight. Every nation who you have made will worship you; because you are great and do wondrous things. I profess that you are God and God alone. Teach me your way, so that I will walk in your truth. My heart will fear your name because to fear you is the beginning of knowledge. Father God, I will praise you with all my heart and I will glorify your name forever. I belong to you for great is your mercy towards me. When I was at my lowest point, you came and delivered my soul. When the enemy desired to destroy me, you strengthened me. I know I don't deserve all this but you are full of compassion and goodness. Manifest your power in me so that others will know I am yours. Thank you, Father for your help and comfort Amen! (Psalm 86.)

Caught up in His Love

"He brought me to the banquet hall. His banner over me is
love." **(Songs of Solomon 2:4)**

*L*ord God, I mediate on your goodness. I read about
you and my heart is glad! Oh how I yearn to be
engulfed in your presence with your glory filling
my temple that I may be as Moses after being in your presence.
You are my God and I am your child. I submit my will to you. I
commit my soul to you. I submit my mind to you. I submit my
heart to you. I give up the grip I have on myself and turn it over
to you. I am in total dependence of you. No matter my frame of
mind or my circumstance you are embedded in me. "You will
guide me with your counsel, and afterward receive me to
glory. Whom do I have in heaven? There is no one on earth
whom I desire besides you. My flesh and my heart fails, but God
is the strength of my heart and my portion forever" (Psalm
73:24-26).

I bless you, Lord, with my soul!! You are very great. You
are clothed with honor and majesty, which covers you with light
a garment, which stretch out the heavens like a curtain. Oh
Sovereign Lord, search me and know me. Remove anything and
everything that is not pleasing in your sight. You are my
strength. You are my light in darkness. You make my crooked
places straight. Your mercy endures forever. You are from
everlasting to everlasting. How or what can I do in order to
advance your Kingdom? What may I do to help complete your
plan? I am available to you, for you, and for your glory. Help me
to remain steadfast in my faith. Draw near to me as I draw near
to you. Be my constant companion, guide, and standard in the
way I live my life and how I treat others. Help me to walk in
love, power, mercy, forgiveness, meekness, joy, longsuffering,
boldness. Let me walk in the anointing of the Holy Spirit. Oh
bless the Lord oh my soul!

Father God, you never fail to put that passion in my heart. I
long for you more and more. Wow! I am so grateful for these
moments. They are very special moments. You are God and God
alone. Where do I go from here with a heart so enlightened and

enlarged of your goodness? I bow in worship to you. My heart is satisfied yet I yearn for more of you. Let me be a sweet fragrance in your nostril. I bless you Lord for all that you are.

Only by His Goodness

"Surely goodness and loving kindness shall follow me all the days of my life, and I will dwell in Yahweh's house forever."
(Psalm 23:6)

*L*ord, God my heart is overwhelmed because of your compassion towards me. I am so grateful for your grace and mercy. I am certainly humbled at your presence. God I just want to lie at your feet and bask in your glory. I just want to worship you and gaze upon your face. Oh Lord God I am in awe of you. My soul yearns for you, totally and fully. Engulf me with your presence. Consume me with your love. Encompass me oh God. I don't want to leave your holy presence. Tears flow from my eyes from the fullness in my heart because of who you are. I will praise you with my whole heart. Jesus, Jesus, Jesus, there is none like you in all the earth! You are my light when I am in darkness. You are my joy in the time of sorrow. You are my peace in the time of trouble. You are my salvation. Here is my heart Lord I give it to you and my life, I lay it down for you because you did that for me. Where else would I go? How deeply I need you, my Lord? Help me to be a woman after your heart.

Mary J. Bryant

I Am the Apple of His Eye

"Keep me as the apple of your eye. Hide me under the shadow of your wings." (Psalm 17:8)

Oh Father, how precious you are to me. You are Sovereign. You loved me enough to send your Son, Jesus, to redeem me back to you. I thank you for your steadfast love. I will be forever faithful to you. I give myself to you more and more each day. Jesus, you have paid the price that only you could pay. You are worthy Lord of all the praise, honor, and glory.

It is my desire that I am pleasing in your sight. Protect me from all that would hurt me, from the temptations that would take me away from you, from desires that lead me to compromise my faith, from harsh criticism, and most of all from the attacks of the evil one. Thank you for loving me and protecting me. Bless me that I may become a blessing to others. As you have established my purpose, order my footsteps to walk in your way.

Lord, there are times when my heart hurts so that it feels as though it will stop beating. However, there are those marvelous times, like today, that I feel my heart growing from your love. It feels like I am coming alive again, like the dawning of a new day. All I can do is think of you, read of you and desire more of you. I am hungry for you Lord God. I don't want to ever lose this feeling I have for you. However, it is more than a feeling it is a relationship. It is like a "Mary" moment when I just want to sit at your feet and worship you, and love on you. Holy Spirit, fall fresh on me. Feed me until I want no more.

Rivers of Living Water: Seek, Knock, Ask

*So I say to you: Ask and it will be given to you; seek and you will
find; knock and the door will be opened to you. If you then,
though you are evil, know how to give good gifts to your
children, how much more will your Father in heaven give the
Holy Spirit to those who ask him!"*
(Luke 11:9, 13 NIV)

*L*ord, I tried not to journal today, but as I listened to
Marvin Sapp singing "I Am Thirsty" made me
realized that you are my living water yet again. I am
reminded that I need you every moment of the day. I do thirst
for you. I do not want to be dry and ineffective on this journey. I
want to grow spiritually and produce much good fruit to your
glory. I want to be a blessing to you and to others. I want to be
an encourager to those who need encouraging. I want to be a
friend to those who are friendless. I want to be effective and
fruitful. My heart is enlarged within. Develop my character by
your Spirit. Give me discernment to judge between good and
evil, right and wrong—in Jesus name. Nothing is hidden from
you. Order and direct my steps Lord God. I need you every step
of the way. You are God and God alone. Bless your name Oh
God. Jesus! Oh God! Oh God! Oh God! How do I make it
without you?

That's Good News

"The LORD your God is with you, the Mighty Warrior who saves. He will take great delight in you; in his love he will no longer rebuke you, but will rejoice over you with singing."
(Zephaniah 3:17 NIV)

I am so grateful to you for your encouragement because there are times when I am confused, like today. When I didn't know what to do and was at the point of giving up, I just seem to be neither here nor there, no direction, and no confidence in my future. It is certainly of great comfort and encouragement to know that you, Lord, are mighty in the midst of me. It is awesome that you rejoice over me with joy and with singing. You are Sovereign. You keep me when I can't keep myself. And I am so grateful to you. I am in your debt. I owe you all that I am or hope to be. I don't know what I would do without you. I am weak, but you are strong.

Thank you for sending the woman of God (Erica Lakin) on Sunday to speak a word to my soul. It was just confirmation. Thank you. I kept seeing me up there—I have preaching and teaching on my mind. I do have a desire for the truth to be taught, and the only way I can do that is by studying your word and by the Spirit of Truth teaching me and giving me revelation by the anointing.

Lord, I just feel so scattered. I thank you for helping me to have a sound mind in the midst of confusion. Thank you for your peace. Help me to keep my mind fixed on Jesus, the author and finisher of my faith. It is you who listen to my prayer and cry for help, and answer me. Thank you for never leaving me or forsaking me.

Thank you for your great mercy toward me. In reverence, I

will bow down toward your feet.

All my help comes from you. You have an expected end for me. Lord I love you because you first loved me. Take me and mold me to your glory and praise. Amen!

Mary J. Bryant

Reverence to a Holy God

"Come, let us bow down in worship, let us kneel before the LORD our Maker" (Psalm 95:6 NIV)

Oh Lord, I acknowledge your Sovereignty. I reverence you as God and Lord of my life. I receive you as Spirit in my life. I cannot do anything without you oh God. I cannot walk right without you. I cannot talk right without you. I cannot see right without you. I cannot hear right without you. I cannot love right without you. I cannot be all you want me to be without you. So I surrender my life over to you. I surrender my will over to you. I yield my weakness to your strength. I release my ways, my mind, my goals, my plans, my shortcomings, my iniquities, presumptuous sins to you right now in the name of Jesus. I give way to the authority of Jesus Christ and the Holy Spirit.

Oh Lord, I cannot make it without you! I need you every step of the way. When I don't know which way to go, when confusion has set in, guide me in what I should do. Order my steps in where I should go to bring peace in the midst of confusion. Oh Lord, when dark clouds come my way, be my light and my salvation. When my enemies even my foes come against me, be my strength and my shield even my buckler and my fortress; be my refuge, be my present help in the time of trouble; let me dwell in your shelter and let me rest in your shadow. Cover me with your arms of protection. For I put my trust in you. You are faithful and your love and mercy endures forever. Morning after morning new mercies I see. Your compassion never fails. Oh Lord God I am so grateful that the Holy Spirit abides in me because I can boldly say "Greater is He that is in me then He who is in the world" (1 John 4:4). Oh God I thank you that even in spite of me, I am the apple of your eye because I am wonderfully and fearfully made by your hands. You rejoice over me with singing. You knew me before I was even a thought to my mother and father. You knew me before time began. Hallelujah! Lord God I thank you because you have thoughts to prosper me and to give me an expected end.

Thank you Lord. I am getting excited just writing to you. I am excited because when I go through the trials and tribulations, you are with me. When I experience the darkest days, I will not be consumed by them because you are my protection. When I feel like I am drowning in my circumstances I will not be destroyed because you shield me. As I go through life's challenges, I will not be fearful for you are with me. I thank you for your protection Lord. Hallelujah - Glory to your name, Father!!

Oh Lord God I thank you right now. I thank you that you are doing a new thing and I will not dwell in the past, but I will forget those former things. As it springs up, oh God, help me to perceive it. Don't let me miss your glory. Give me eyes to see and ears to hear. I don't want to walk in my own understanding, but in all my ways I want to acknowledge you so that you and only you will direct my path. I seek your kingdom and everything else will be added unto me. Give me wisdom that I may walk in your way. Help me get understanding so I may be able to boldly speak as I should speak in all truth and love in Jesus name. Hallelujah - Glory to Your name, Oh God!!

The Love of the Lord leaves Me Speechless

"But God commends his own love toward us, in that while we were yet sinners, Christ died for us." (Romans 5:8)

Father, it is just so amazing how you care for me. I am at a loss for words to describe all of your goodness and mercy (love). All I can truly say is to God be the glory! It was very hard for me yesterday. But because I put my trust in you, I was able to hold on. As I cried out to you, you were right there by my side. I don't know what tomorrow may bring, but I cling to you. I need you every step of the way. There is no decision I want to make without you. There is no where I want to go without you leading me. There is nothing I want to say without you giving me the words. My life no longer belongs to me. It belongs to you. Make me useful for your purpose. I don't even want to think with my mind, but let my mind be like the mind of Christ Jesus. Lord God, thank you for always being here for me.

Father, you bless me beyond measure. I am in the over flow of your blessings. You keep me from falling. As I remain in you, I will bare much fruit for your glory. Increase my passion and desire to study your Scriptures. I want to be guided and directed by God, the Holy Spirit, that I may know your truth by revelation knowledge. Your revealed knowledge where my mind is renewed and I can be transformed into the image and likeness of Jesus. Let your glory rest on me so that others will be drawn to your presence.

I know life will have its ups and downs. But because I am yours, I will continually praise you. You are God! I am learning how to be content in whatever state I find myself.

No One Can Love Me Like Jesus!

*"I am the good shepherd. The good shepherd lays down his life for the sheep." **(John 10:11)***

Oh how I love Jesus because He first loved me. My soul cries out hallelujah! How I yearn for you. I desire to know the power of your resurrection and becoming more like you. I am so overjoyed in you, LORD! I need you every day and every way. Lord, help me not to fall away from you. Give me more of you that I will become less of me. I desire your knowledge, wisdom and understanding.

I can do without anything but I cannot do without you. You are my life, the breath of my very existence. You are never weak. You are never tired. You never sleep or slumber. You never give way to confusion. When I am weak, I come to you and you make me strong because your strength is made perfect in my weakness. When I am tired, you give me rest. When I grow weary, you lift me up. You give me joy in the midst of my sadness for your joy is my strength.

I will wait for you and you will strengthen my heart. There is no one like you, Lord.

Mary J. Bryant

Surrendered to His Will: Under Reconstruction

*"We know that all things work together for good for those who
love God, to those who are called according to his purpose."*
(Romans 8:28)

Still proclaiming and declaring you are Sovereign God. You deserve all the honor and praise. I worship you in all your majesty and splendor. I thank you God for loving me. Although this is the day that you have made, I find myself down in my spirit and cast down in my soul. I am consumed with the cares of this life. I ask myself why I should feel this way when I am more than a conqueror through Christ Jesus. I am blessed when I go and when I come. I am the daughter of Abraham by faith. Why I am down casted concerning the cares of this life? You are greater than anything I may be going through. Why do I feel alone in the world when you are always with me? Why do I feel incomplete when I am complete in you? You are the head of all principality, and power. Why should I have unhealthy thoughts when I have the mind of you, Christ? Why do I feel confused when I have the peace of you, God, which passes all understanding? Why do I feel powerless when I have received power from the Holy Spirit? Why do I feel like a miss-fit when I am your workmanship, created in Christ? Why do I feel defeated when I am an overcomer, by the blood of the Lamb, and the word of my testimony? Why do I feel like I am always behind everyone else when I am the head and not the tail? Why do I feel unloved when I am greatly loved by you, God? Why do I feel weak when I am strengthened with all might according to your glorious power? Why do I feel shaken by what I see or feel, when I am firmly rooted, built up, established in my faith and overflowing with gratitude? Why am I timid when you have not given me the spirit

96

of fear but of power, love and a sound mind? Oh Lord, only you know what's best for me. You are the potter and I am the clay, use me for your service. I surrender to your will.

Realization Because of Revelation

"That the God of our Lord Jesus Christ, the Father of glory, may give to you a spirit of wisdom and revelation in the knowledge of him" (Ephesians 1:17)

ord, I am compelled to write to you at this very moment. My soul chases hard after you. I have such a reverence for you. I am in awe of who you are. Your greatness and majesty humbles me. I have been in counsel concerning healing and sickness. It has been very interesting. May the Spirit of wisdom and revelation be given to know you better. May there be freedom from any outside restrictions, any hindrance or any bondage that may keep me from doing what you would have me to do. Give me that bold spirit to speak as I ought to, as the Spirit gives me utterance. Let my confidence be in you and not in "Mary". I can't do anything without you. I do depend on you to lead and guide me and to be my, Jehovah Jireh, my Provider.

Yearning to be in His Presence

"As the deer pants for the water brooks, so my soul pants after you, God.**" (Psalm 42:1)**

*I*nhaling deeply, as I drove to work this morning, I turned off my radio. I just wanted to listen for your voice Lord. Yesterday you visited me and I wanted the same thing today. I ask these questions of you God and of myself:

1. What do I do when I am not hearing from you?
2. What do I say when you don't tell me what to say?
3. Where do I go if you don't lead me?
4. What can I do if you don't tell me what to do?
5. How can I live without you living in me?

Oh how I yearn for you in my lowest valley and my highest mountain. I just want to cleave to you and receive your Holy Spirit, to know the mysteries of the Kingdom. You are so precious to me; your presence is so very sweet. Your words are so comforting. I don't ever want to be without your presence. It is your face I seek. I feel so full right now as I love you more and more. You are so compassionate towards me and you are forever faithful. It's very amazing, how such a holy God as you, love me so much. Before I received Jesus as Savior and Lord, I was not worthy to untie your shoes. Please instruct my heart. Impart in me an inward hunger and thirst for your truth. Grant me the divine anointing so I may behold that which is invisible to the natural eye. I close my eyes to float away to your throne just so I can worship you.

"Do not fear, Mary. Do not let your hands hang limp. I am with you, I will save you. I take great delight in you. I will quiet you with my love. I will rejoice over you with singing. Mary, I will deal with all who oppress you. I will give you praise and honor". (Zephaniah 3:16-20 NIV).

Mary J. Bryant

Be Still

*"For you shall not go out in haste, neither shall you go by flight:
for Yahweh will go before you; and the God of Israel will be
your rear guard." (Isaiah 52:12)*

*"Don't you be afraid, for I am with you. Don't be dismayed, for I
am your God. I will strengthen you. Yes, I will help you. Yes, I
will uphold you with the right hand of my righteousness."
(Isaiah 41:10)*

As I struggle through this test of my faith, I sense you speaking to me Father. I believe you want me to walk by faith and not by sight. I should wait on you to deliver me and lead me in the way of your peace. I know you have not forgotten about me.

I surrender to your love you have for me. Help me to sit calmly as my anxious thoughts try to take my focus off you. I depend on the measure of faith that you gave me to help me rest in you. Help me to not move ahead of your will. Give me your grace to count the most difficult challenges the greatest blessings.

Thank you for holding me in your righteous right hand. You told me to sit still and you would fight my battles. Thank you for being my stronghold in my present struggle.

Just for Who You Are

*"Holy, holy, holy is the Lord God Almighty, who was, and is, and is to come." **(Revelation 4:8)***

*J*ust let me love on you Lord. You are Sovereign and I praise you because you reign, Lord. I humble myself to the only wise, eternal, and living God. Oh how I bow before you to worship you, to behold you and reverence your holiness. You are God and God alone. I meditate on your greatness and your goodness.

You created the heaven and the earth. You don't need any one or anything to exist. You are holy and sovereign. Your sovereignty is over your creation. You are unchangeable, unshakable and unstoppable. You are God by yourself. No one can compare to you. You are the supreme authority and power. You are not subject to any human authority or power. No human can stop your plan. You know the end before the beginning because you are Alpha and Omega.

I worship you in the beauty of who you are. You are holy. The angels even worship before your throne. I praise you just for who you are. You have done enough to receive all glory, praise and honor. No one will escape from bowing down in reverence to your name. I cry holy, holy, holy to the Lamb of God!

Humbled Because of Who He Is

"For great is Yahweh, and greatly to be praised! He is to be feared above all gods." **(Psalm 96:4)**

s I am reading my email, *Back to the Bible Lessons*, I am falling in love with you even more. I am humbled as I read about you. I want to just love on you and lay at your feet reverencing your Sovereignty. My heart is enlarged because of you. My body is exhausted and need rest, but I just need and want to meditate on your goodness. I take a deep breathe, inhaling you into me. I consider my life no longer mine but yours. Use me as you will. I am yielded to you. It's my heart's desire to do what pleases you. My life is surrendered to you. At this very moment I can't think of anything more I would rather do than to be obedient to you. I am overwhelmed and in awe of you. Draw me, Lord. Abide in me and me in you. Let your glory be revealed in me, that others may come to you in repentance and accept Jesus as their savior and Lord, believing by faith that Jesus is the Son of the true and living God. Who has been raised from the dead and now He is seated at your right hand and all power has been given unto Him. There is power in your name, Jesus.

My Praise Outweighs My Pain

"Yahweh is my rock, my fortress, and my deliverer; my God, my rock, in whom I take refuge; my shield, and the horn of my salvation, my high tower." (Psalm 18:2)

While driving to work this morning, I had no strength, no energy, and no motivation. I felt like I was just existing, nothing to look forward to. Then this song about praising God came on and my spirit came alive with praise for the great God I love. I realized no matter how great my struggles may be, how weary I am, how heartbroken I am or how emotionally neglected I am, my praise outweighs my pain. When the enemy comes to put condemnation on me, it is a lie. I know what the Lord God has done for me. I know how He covered me when Satan came to destroy me. He protected me when the devil tried to get a stronghold over my mind. He came to bury me in a hole of darkness and torment me, but God said "no". His love kept me through it all and it keeps me every day of my life. I know I can't make it without you Lord God. I need your anointing that destroys every yoke, and sets the captives free.

As I go through these tests, trials, and tribulations, I am emptied of all my strength. I have come to the end of Mary, so you can step in and take me from strength to strength. Before you can be who you are in my life, I have to be weakened. In other words, all my natural strength in divine things is powerless. In order to learn this I need trials that are so great that my own strength is insufficient to bear them. I must have temptations where my strength against them is powerless. I have to believe by faith, to trust in you God, and the work that Christ did on the cross and the power of the Holy Spirit. This brings a discovery of your majesty, purity and holiness. I had to sink down into ruin, hopelessness, and helplessness in order to give up the idea of depending on my strength. By nature we are creatures of independence and self-centeredness.

It has taken me years of trials to come to knowing your strength is made perfect when I am weak. I believe your grace is enough for me. Through trial after trial, temptation after temptation, and affliction after affliction, I have learned the secret to my weakness. Out of this experience, the Holy Spirit revealed that I must put my trust in you. God, you are the strength of my heart and my portion forever. God said to Apostle Paul, "My grace is sufficient for you, for my power is made perfect in weakness" (2 Corinthians 12:9).

My praise outweighs my pain. I have a well of water in me springing to everlasting life. It is a well of divine refreshments, gracious manifestations, and heavenly testimonies. All from the God who comforts, blesses, and waters the soul and makes it like a watered garden.

This well is hidden from unseeing eyes. In the midst of my sorrows, trials and temptations, God's mercies are new each morning. I know every time I find myself in that familiar place of darkness where Satan is seeking to steal, kill, destroy, or where I am being pruned to produce more fruit, there is a refreshing, a strengthening, and a comforting for my soul. Though I face temptations, I've been given strength to bear them. I have had trials but I have been given grace to endure them. I have had persecution but I have been given support to overcome them. I have had heart-rending afflictions, but the Lord has not allowed me to be destroyed by them. I have had secret strength communicated to my soul. I have leaned on an unseen arm, and have found support in visible realities.

"For the LORD God is a sun and shield; the LORD bestows favor and honor; no good thing does he withhold from those whose walk is blameless" (Psalm 84:11 NIV).

He Deserves the Glory, the Honor and the Praise

*"Yahweh is our God. Yahweh is one. ⁵ You shall love
Yahweh your God with all your heart, with all your soul, and
with all your might." (Deuteronomy 6:4-5)*

ather, I love you with all my heart and with all my
soul and with all my might so that I will be pleasing
to you. Put me on the Potter's wheel to mold me. My
heart opens up to you. Sanctify me to yourself. I don't want it to
be no other way for me. There is no other choice for me. There is
no other answer for me. It is you and only you. I choose your
will and your way. Oh make me fully yours. I want to be fully
obedient to you and fully trusting you by faith, a progressive
faith. My soul needs to be fed by you. I open wide my mouth so
pour in me, touch my tongue with coal like you did with Isaiah.
Put your word in my mouth like you did with Jeremiah and
Ezekiel. You are my life and the center of my existence. Come,
Lord Jesus, move upon my mind, my heart, my soul in such a
radical way that your glory radiates my very being. I will
become a change agent for Christ, having such a sweet Spirit
upon me. Let your revealed glory in me honor your Holy name.

I fall in love with you more and more. Every time I read
or think about how good and merciful you are towards me, my
heart gives way to love and reverence. I want all who don't
know you, to come to know you and love you Father. Help me
share and convey your Good News; your message of salvation in
its fullness. I rest in the cleft of your bosom. I'm longing for
your presence. As I come near to you, come near to me. Let your
Holy Spirit come upon me so that I may worship you in Spirit
and in Truth that I may see the wonders in your word.

*"But when he, the Spirit of truth, comes, he will guide you
into all the truth. He will not speak on his own; he will speak
only what he hears, and he will tell you what is yet to come"
(John 16:13 NIV).*

Does my hunger for you please you? Does my thirst please you? Satisfy both my hunger and thirst as only you can. You are my well spring of life.

Secret Place

*"He who dwells in the secret place of the Most High will rest in the shadow of the Almighty." **(Psalm 91:1)***

Call me into your secret chamber that we may have fellowship and sweet communion together. And I may be changed into the image of Christ and live a life that is pleasing to you. I want to honor you and worship you in Spirit and in Truth. I am continually pursuing you to seek your face and to be in your presence. I want to sit at your feet and learn from you. I want your most excellent way and most precious gifts. I want the best you have. I give you thanksgiving and praise, being mindful and humbled at all times. Search my heart and know me. See if there is any wicked way in me and remove it. Wash me with hyssop that I may be clean and made whole. That I may stand before you with clean hands and a pure heart.

I sigh because I want to be caught up in your presence. I search for my place in you so I can know your purpose for me. There is such a void in me, longing for you to uncover the treasure you have in me. Not for my glory but for your glory. I will lift up the name of Jesus and you will do the drawing, not by my might or power but by your Spirit. I want my heart to be sensitive to your voice so I am always obedient to you. Help my heart to discern between good and evil. Oh God, I worship you, Almighty God! I worship you, Prince of Peace. God I give you glory because you are my righteousness. There is none like you. No one else can touch my heart like you do. Oh my! I love you because you first loved me.

You call me into your secret place where we commune together. The fellowship we have is sweet to me. Nothing else matters when I am in your presence. When I am in your presence, I get refreshed. I meditate on your goodness day and night.

"Give thanks to the LORD for his unfailing love and his wonderful deeds for mankind, for he satisfies the thirsty and fills the hungry with good things" (Psalm 107:8-9 NIV).

Brought Out to Be Brought In: Out of Darkness into His Marvelous Light

*"But you are a chosen race, a royal priesthood, a holy nation, a people for God's own possession, that you may proclaim the excellence of him who called you out of darkness into his marvelous light." (**1 Peter 2:9**)*

*"See how great a love the Father has given to us, that we should be called children of God! For this cause the world doesn't know us, because it didn't know him. ² Beloved, now we are children of God, and it is not yet revealed what we will be. But we know that, when he is revealed, we will be like him; for we will see him just as he is." (**1 John 3:1-2**)*

Oh how I love God because He first loved me. The love of God makes me His child. In the natural, children have features and ways of their parents. Being that God is my Spiritual Father; I want to have His ways. I want to look like Him. I want to talk like Him. I want to love like Him. I want to give like Him. I want to forgive like Him. I want to be all that He wants me to be and accomplish all that He has planned for me to do.

Lord, you have examined me and know all about me. You know when I sit down and when I get up. You know my thoughts before I think them. You know when I get up and when I lie down. You know thoroughly everything I do. LORD, even before I say a word, you already know it. You are all around me, in front and in back, you have put your hand on me. Your knowledge is amazing to me; it is more than I can understand. You made my whole being. You formed me in my mother's body. I praise you because you made me in an amazing and wonderful way. What you have done is wonderful. I know this very well.

109

All the days planned for me were written in your book before I was one day old. God, your thoughts are precious to me. They are too numerous for me to count. When I wake up I am still with you and you are still with me. Thank you for always being with me.

Giver of Every Good and Perfect Gift

"With God is my salvation and my honor. The rock of my strength, and my refuge, is in God. Trust in him at all times, you people. Pour out your heart before him. God is a refuge for us. Selah." **(Psalm 62:7-8)**

am meditating on your goodness Lord, knowing that every good and perfect gift comes from you. You even make all things work for my good. My heart is overwhelmed with praise and I honor your majesty. I reverence and worship your sovereignty. There is no other god like you, Lord. You reign above every king and your kingdom surpasses all other kingdoms. Your power rules over all other power and principalities. You are the great I Am, yet you still loved me enough to give your life for me so I could have eternal life. I am humbled because of it. Thank You!

Your servant and friend listen to hear and obey your voice. Let my heart be circumcised by your Holy Spirit, so I will be pleasing in your sight and bring your glory. There is such praise in my heart for you. Let it overflow with singing, shouting, dancing, that it will reach heaven. Draw your people into your presence to praise you, honestly and sincerely, knowing that you deserve all the praise. You inhabit the praises of your people.

Please keep me as the apple of your eye. Don't be far from me. Draw me to you.

I bless you because you give me counsel; in the night my heart instructs me. I have set you always before me, because you are at my right hand and I shall not be shaken (Psalm 16:7-8). **Come Lord Jesus!**

Mary J. Bryant

When Truth Meets Error

"You will know the truth, and the truth will make you free."
(John 8:32)

heard the statement "You are so heavenly-minded
to you are no earthly good." I would often wonder
what they were talking about because it really
didn't make too much sense to me. Then one day I was
enlightened by the Holy Spirit after reading Colossians 3:2 "Set
your mind on things above not on things on the earth." I am
having a divine moment with the Holy Spirit. I feel a fresh
anointing in me and over me. I bless the Lord at all times. Bless
the LORD O my soul and all that is in me Bless His holy name. I
forget not His benefits: He has forgiven all my iniquities. You
heal all my sickness (diseases). You redeemed my life from
destruction. You crown me with loving kindness and tender
mercies. You satisfy my mouth with good things so that my
youth is renewed like the eagle's (Psalm 103). I bless you, Lord.
You are my strength and shield. It is you that I trust.

With you I can face all my giants, because all things are
possible with you. This is the day that you have made and I am
rejoicing in it. My soul is glad in you. Thank you so much for
this very day with you! My heart has been enlarged with your
love, your divine, everlasting love. I am being blessed - my
blessings are overflowing and I want to share it. Let my
blessings flow to whomever you would send my way.

This has been a wonderfully glorious time with you this
morning. It is almost 12 noon and time was not a concern to me
today. I am just enjoying the move of your Holy Spirit on my
heart. Give me more of you, Lord. My spirit is overwhelmed.
My soul thirsts for you. Thank you for your loving kindness. It
causes me to live the way I should. Continue to teach me to do

112

your will. I want to be pleasing in your sight. Continue to pour out your Holy Spirit in me that I will be changed from the inside out, changing me into your image and likeness day by day, that I may bring glory to you and honor to your throne. Thank you for you! I am so very grateful for your divine visitation! I asked and you gave more than I imagined.

Mary J. Bryant

When Nothing Else Will Do

"Let your Kingdom come. Let your will be done, as in
heaven, so on earth. Give us today our daily bread."
(Matthew 6:10-11)

I lay and cry before you Father, yearning for a closer
and deeper relationship with you as my creator, my
God, my Father, my redeemer, my Lord, my friend.
Your statues stand firm; holiness adorns your house for endless
days, O LORD (Psalm 93:5). Help me to build my life on a
secure and sure foundation. Fill me with the Holy Spirit to bring
forth the fruit of the Spirit in me so that I will show your grace
and your character. Give me a renewed hunger to know your will
and to seek your truth. Help me understand your will and apply it
in my life. I want my life to be built with you at the center and
the head. You know the way I should take. I want Christ to dwell
in my heart through faith and that I am rooted and grounded in
love (Ephesian 3:17). Keep me from straying from your path of
righteousness and love.

Oh God cover me with your peace. Keep me grounded in
you, heavenly Father. I don't want any other spirit to have
control over me except the Holy Spirit. Lord, I am weak but you
are strong and mighty. Let your power come upon this weak
vessel that I may take courage and not give up or turn back. You
are faithful and I want to be faithfully full of integrity. My goal
is to become more like you, in image and likeness. I want to be
pleasing in your sight.

Hold me in the palm of your hand. You are my refuge and
my fortress. Your truth is my shield. I have made you my Lord.
You have become by habitation. I shall not be afraid of evil
spirited people who try to harm me. It doesn't matter how many

or how few come against me, they will not harm me. You have given your angels to keep me safe. You, Lord will satisfy me with long life and show me your salvation. I give thanks to you Lord God. I praise you for you are a great King above all gods. I come to bow down and worship you, my LORD, and my maker. I want to know your ways so that I won't err in my heart but enter your rest. Heavenly Father, I declare your glory, for you are great, and greatly to be praised. You are to be feared above all gods. I worship you in the beauty of holiness.

I love your Word. I want understanding. Help me keep your ways. I desire to have good judgment. Let my heart be sound (blameless) that I won't be ashamed. Be my guide so that sin won't have dominion over me.

I love you Jesus! Jesus I love you! You are my source of life. I cling to you Jesus because you are the lover of my soul. I am engulfed with my thoughts and yearning of you. I want to be in your presence, to hear your voice speaking to me. Come to me even now. Hold me with your everlasting loving arms. Draw me close to your bosom that I am one with you, your breath and your heart beat. Oh how I need you more and more. The more I think about you the more I need you. Set my soul to flight by your Spirit, that I am not a caged bird beating my wings on the bars that contain and restrain me. My yearning for you and my burning desire is to do work in your Kingdom for your glory. I do not want to rush your perfect work in me. I want to walk in your authority and power to be effective in the Kingdom and for the Kingdom. I give glory to your Name, Father. I Praise your name for your goodness. You are the Most High God. You have been with me every step of the way leading me, guiding me, protecting, teaching, correcting me. You are truly my Shepherd. Although I am writing what is in my heart, I don't want to stop because it is a down pour from heaven and I am overflowing with the love of God.

I am looking to be in my place one day Lord where I can share that which you have given to me. I am rich beyond measure and want to share it with others in Jesus name. Let the people be hungry and receive your word. I could write about what is plaguing me but I would rather write about my Redeemer and how good you are to me. Not that I have been so faithful or so good but you are God. Jesus I love you! Jesus I love you because you care. Wonderful Jesus! Wonderful Master! I bow down and worship at your feet. I reverence you. Teach me to fear your name more and more. Thank you for the drawing from you Father and setting me on the right road to salvation. Thank You! When no one else cared for my soul; when no one else desired to be around me, I cried unto you and you heard my cry. You delivered me! Thank you. When I was lonely, you became my friend. In my sickness, you brought healing. When I was left out and pushed aside, and rejected, you accepted me into your family. Thank you. You turned my disappointments into your appointments. You even turned my obstacles into opportunities. Praise God! My mouth shall speak the praise of the LORD. Let all flesh bless your name forever and ever, in Jesus name, Amen.

There is Wisdom in the Fear of the Lord

"Only fear Yahweh, and serve him in truth with all your heart;
for consider what great things he has done for you."
(1 Samuel 12:24)

ather, teach me to fear your name and serve you in truth with my marvelously and awesomely wonderful. You are holy and deserve to be feared, honored, worshipped, adored, exalted, praised, served, loved, obeyed, followed, and trusted. My hope is in you because you saved us from destruction!

Father, you have provided every spiritual blessing in Christ Jesus and in Jesus is where I need to be. It is in Christ I sit in heavenly places. I am chosen in Christ. I am adopted through Christ. I am accepted in the Beloved [Christ]. I am redeemed in Christ. I am given an inheritance in Christ. I am given hope in Christ. I am sealed in Christ. I am made alive together with Christ. I am raised and seated with Christ. I am a partaker of the promise in Christ. I am given access through faith in Him.

Father, I am your workmanship, created in Christ Jesus. Help me to know my purpose. Help me to walk in your way. In Jesus name I pray.

I want to honor You Father by being more discipline in all I do. I want to walk in excellence by receiving your best. That is why I want to learn and practice to stay in Christ because in Christ I am rich beyond measure. I want my spiritual walk to be rooted in your spiritual wealth. What else is there? Nothing can compare to my Savior Jesus Christ. In Christ I am complete. In Christ I have everything I need. In Christ I am everything God has purposed me to be. Praise God! Thank you Jesus!

Father, I love the sweet communion of the Holy Spirit!! I

want to always be lead and filled by your Holy Spirit. I don't want any other spirit to have charge over me, except for the Spirit of the true and living God. This is my confession and my declaration.

My Shepherd

"I rejoice at your word, as one who finds great plunder."
(Psalm 119:162)

I sometimes go through difficulties and people may lie on me and uncomfortable situations may rise. People may not like me and I am misunderstood and criticized. Nevertheless, the Lord my God is with me and He pleads and defends my case. He is my heavenly advocate and my High Priest. His grace still abounds in my life. Even in the midst of my struggles, I know He is right here with me. My body is saturated with aches and pains. As I am going through my day, my body is struggling to carry me. I believe God is a healer and He can provide the cure for whatever is coming against my body. I trust Him to do what He says He will do on my behalf.

Even people seem to want to surround me with negative vibes. They are not people of honor and integrity. They will use you and smile in your face, but all the while they don't like you and will stab you in your back. Still God is for me and if God is for me who can be against me. They walk in darkness but I walk in God's light. He is my protection and no one can harm me because I abide under the shadows of the Almighty, the Most High God. No one or nothing can take me from His powerful right hand. Glory to God! When I am weak, His strength is made perfect. So I am still so very grateful to my King and my Lord. I am glad that I am under His rule and not of the ruler of this world. I am a child of the King and have citizenship in His Kingdom, which is forever. Praise God! There is no other god like Him. No other god before Him or after Him. I take delight in knowing and believing and trusting that He has all power, all knowledge, and all sight to see all. I am glad He chose me and now I have chosen Him. Bless His name. I will yet praise my worthy King. He has set my feet upon a solid rock to stand. I am complete in Christ. Father, continue to provide so that I will come into the fullness of all that I am in Christ. Help me to continue to live my life to honor, praise and worship you. Help me to submit myself all the more to your will. I desire to do your will and your work. Help me to carry Your Word in my heart and to speak it out of my mouth with all holiness and purity of heart. I don't want to speak from the strength of Mary or by my opinion but let me rightly divide Your Word of Truth so I won't be ashamed or bring dishonor to you or lead others astray. I do take this very seriously. I want to be known by you because of my love for you and how it builds up and not tear down. Let love not only be the first thing but let it be the true foundation on which I do and say all things. Keep this in my mind as I do your will as your servant. As I surrender to be your bond servant, I want to know that I am your friend as Jesus called his disciples. There is a difference in being a servant and friend.

"You are my friends, if you do whatever I command you. No longer do I call you servants, for the servant doesn't know what his lord does. But I have called you friends, for everything that I heard from my Father, I have made known to you.
(John 15:14-15).

I desire your best. Grant it unto me according to your will. You are my Lord and my Master. I need you always and in every way.

Morning after Morning New Mercies Come

"Who is a God like you, who pardons iniquity, and passes over the disobedience of the remnant of his heritage? He doesn't retain his anger forever, because he delights in loving kindness."
(Micah 7:18)

h thank you for delighting in mercy. If it had not been for your great love that produces grace and mercy I would be destroyed and separated from you. Father, you are my creator, my King, my Savior, my LORD, my life. You have redeemed and restored me back to the Father. You have justified me, just as if I have never sinned. You wrap me in your righteousness. It was you who suffered for me. You gave your life for me through your blood. You became a sacrifice that I may have peace (Shalom) with God, the Father. Oh how I thank you. No one else could have paid such a price. How can I fully thank you for what you have done? I give you this life you have given me to be used for you according to your will. I count it a humbling privilege and honor to serve you, to be called your child, to be joint heir with Christ, and to be your temple. Because I love you, let the Holy Spirit led me so I may glorify you. I rejoice because of the peace I have at this very moment with you. Thank you oh Holy One of Israel. I worship and adore you LORD. I can imagine how King David must have felt when the Spirit came upon him and he danced out of his kingly garment. Oh Glory!

I love this free move of the Holy Spirit. This is truly a supernatural high I am on. Thank God. I praise you.

First Peter 4:11 states, "If anyone speaks, let it be as it were the very words of God. If anyone serves, let it be as of the strength which God supplies, that in all things God may be glorified through Jesus Christ, to whom belong the glory and the dominion forever and ever. Amen." The song says: All for His glory! I do it all for His glory! Shout glory! Amen! Amen! Amen!

Keeping the Lord Ever before Me

"Simon Peter answered him, "Lord, to whom would we go? You have the words of eternal life." (John 6:68)

My mind is on those things of God. He is showing and teaching me so much. I am a computer and He is downloading all this information on the inside of me, on my hard drive (my heart). Now I have to trust Him to help me share it. I take no confidence in my flesh or my strength or power to unpack it the way it needs to be and how it needs to be. I need His Spirit to carry out His purpose. Help me Lord Jesus.

I was reading Exodus 33 on yesterday. Moses went to the tent of meeting to talk with God. Moses said to God, "You say you know me by name and I have found grace in your sight. Show me the way that I may know you and find grace in your sight. Don't carry us from this place if you aren't going with us." Moses knew that the presence of God would separate them from the world. So Moses wanted to see God's glory - His goodness.

As I searched for God to reveal Himself to me, I remember trying to visualize or imagine how that must have been for Moses. I remember asking God to show me His glory. I just knew I wanted what God had for my life so I could hear Him as Moses did. I too understand that I need God's presence to go with me wherever I go. I need His presence to separate me from the world.

The Spirit descended on Jesus and remained. I desire that also. I want Him to remain on me and in me. I want to decrease so He will increase. I just know I need Him deeply and greatly. I take myself down low so He can be exalted in my life. Everything I desire is wrapped and anchored in pleasing God. I don't want to have anything God doesn't want me to have. I trust

123

God to provide me exactly what I need. He is my creator, but moreover He is my Abba Father. He has never failed me and I don't want to fail Him. I want to be pleasing in every way before Him. He is so faithful and I want to be faithful to Him.

Father, help me to be faithful, obedient, forgiving, loving, kind, gentle, compassionate, self-controlled and thankful. Help me to be all those things that are true, pure, praise worthy, honorable, excellent, and lovely so I can be pleasing in your sight. I think of your word both night and day.

Come Jesus!

"The Spirit and the bride say, "Come!" He who hears, let him say, "Come!" He who is thirsty, let him come. He who desires, let him take the water of life freely."
(Revelation 22:17)

hank you Jesus! Come! I need you every moment of the day. I do come asking, seeking, and knocking. As I was in communion and fellowship with God, I began asking for more of the Holy Spirit and God's grace to be all I should be.

Oh Lord, God Jehovah, you reign! Make me your sanctuary, pure and holy, tried and true. I want to be a living sanctuary for you! Live in my heart that I may know good from evil and be obedient to your voice. I want to always honor you and never sin against you. Oh bless your name. I feel your holy presence. I decrease that you may increase more and more. I surrender; according to the free will you have given me. I surrender my all to you, knowing you are the Potter. Mold me and have free course with Mary. You are my creator and my Father and you have the blue print and the manual for my life. Come and let me take freely of the water of life that it will spring up like rivers of living water. Jesus said that if any man thirsts for Him, come and drink and believing rivers of living water will flow out his belly. Jesus has been glorified and the Spirit is given freely to them that believe. Oh I believe, Jesus!

Oh how I love you Jesus. Thank you for the promised Holy Spirit. And after that you shall receive power and signs and wonders will follow me because I believe (Mark 16:17). In Jesus name, by His authority, I will cast out demons; I shall speak with new tongues; I will take up serpents and if I drink any deadly thing it shall not hurt me; I shall lay hands on the sick and they shall recover. Amen! I believe it!

Open me up to the revelation of your Word that my faith will grow in my knowledge of you. Let me be a motivation unto transformation: from sinners to saints, from desiring the milk of the word to desiring the meat of the word; from the old to the new; from a citizen of the world to a citizen of the Kingdom; from a son of disobedient to a son of obedience; from a child of darkness to a child of light; from unrighteousness to righteousness; from faith to faith and strength to strength. Oh Lord I thank you! You give freely to them that seek, ask, and knock. The Holy Spirit is so precious to me. I don't want to grieve Him. Have full reign Spirit of the living God. I belong to you and you belong to me. Sanctify me into your service all for your glory. I want to be a part of that Prophetic generation who carry your word.

How marvelous are your works and I am one of them. I am humbled that you chose me to be a vessel for your Spirit to dwell. It is as though I am heralded by the angel, as Mary was on that great day. So I say as Mary did in Luke 1:46: "My soul does magnify the Lord, and my spirit has rejoiced in God my Savior. For He has regarded the low estate of His hand maiden; for He that is mighty has done to me great things and holy is His name."

Father, my desire is that you give me the Spirit of wisdom and the fear of the Lord. I ask for the Spirit of revelation. I welcome the fullness of your Holy Spirit. Grant this to me that I might know Jesus more intimately. Grace me with your presence so that I may know you beyond informational knowledge.

Fill me with your glorious presence so that I will know the hope of my calling that I may walk in your purpose and destiny in my life. Grace me so that I may be in touch with the rich deposit of your glorious inheritance placed within me, as I am now a temple of the Holy Spirit. I declare that there will be many deposits and withdrawals out of this treasure chest.

Father I want your light to flood my being so that I will not walk in darkness. Shape me into a faith believer.

Mary J. Bryant

The Capacity to Grow in Grace

"But grow in the grace and knowledge of our Lord and Savior Jesus Christ. To him be the glory both now and forever. Amen."
(2 Peter 3:18)

ather, I was moved not to only write but to get into the word. I was beginning to feel empty and things were beginning to irritate me. So thank you because you are my food. Just like a car needs to be refilled with gas when it's empty or running low, spiritual persons have to refill their spirits with the word of God when they begin feeling more connected to the world then with God. So here I am, fill me until I over flow, running over to others.

I was reading different scriptures on having a gentle spirit. The verse that stood out to me was First Peter 3:15 "But in your hearts revere Christ as Lord. Always be prepared to give an answer to everyone who asks you to give the reason for the hope that you have. But do this with gentleness and respect (NIV)" There are times when it is not always easy for me to present a gentle spirit. However, I can choose to have a gentle spirit. God's word is powerful and alive and He has given us the character of Jesus through the fruit of the Spirit. Galatians 5:22-23 gives us the nine fruit of the Spirit and gentleness is one of them. When allowed to operate, these characteristics direct me in every area of my life. After reading through these verses, I realize that I have been given peace by my Father and my victory is already won. I just have to thank Him for the peace and victory and live it out.

So I pray for a gentle spirit from within so I will remain in your peace. Whenever I am faced with a conflict, or the like, I can keep my character the fruit of the Spirit. Amen! Father gentleness is one of the fruit of the Spirit. It is a characteristic of Jesus and I want it and need it to be pleasing in your sight. You have shown me, I believe, love, patience, self-control, faithfulness, peace, kindness and now gentleness. You are making me into the very image and likeness of Christ. Thank you. Please continue to mold and shape me into the image and likeness of Christ Jesus, your only begotten Son.

I love you Lord because you first loved me. I adore you because you are God. I enter into a state of worship when I think about you. My thoughts become meditations about you. My heart floods with your love for me and my love for you grows and grows. It changes my being on the inside. I can feel the spiritual transformation going on in my heart and pure love and devotion is the result. Keep me rooted and grounded in you. Grant me my heart's desire as I delight myself in you. All glory, praise and honor belong to you.

I can only imagine how the Prophet Isaiah felt when he saw you sitting on your throne or when Stephen saw you standing on the right hand of the Father. If my eyes could ever behold such magnificent and majestic sight in this earthly body, how blessed and humbled I would be.

I want the deeper things of God, not to bring me fame or attention, but because I want all God has purposed for me. I want to see the potential that was hidden in me from before the foundation of the world. I want the best God has for me, not 30, or 60 fold, but 100 fold.

Help me Jesus! Hear my heart's Desire

I ncline your ear to me. Show yourself as Lord of my life. Take me and reconstruct me for your own. You have redeemed me and called me by name. Here I am Lord, your servant hears you, let it be as you say. I accept you as authority, ruler, and King over my life. You formed me and made me fearfully and wonderfully and you know the way I should take. I am yours 100%. I really and truly want to be *souled* out to you. I want to breathe Jesus, inhaling and exhaling. I want my mind to be saturated with thoughts of Jesus. I want to see Him in all that I see; hear Him in all that I hear, give me Jesus! (More than fortune, fame, houses, cars and the like). Jesus is my life, a true treasure indeed, the rarest of jewels. Oh give me Jesus more than anything. Amen.

Thank you Jesus! I know you are here with me. Holy Spirit, fill me to overflowing so others to share your presence.

I have to stop and close my eyes just to think on the goodness of my Lord for a moment before I continue.

This is good, so very good! My heart does burn with your consuming fire. Oh bless your wonderful name filled with splendor and glory. Praise the Lord. Don't want to leave this moment. I want to receive all of what you have for me.

The Truth and Nothing but the Truth

"Your righteousness is an everlasting righteousness. Your law is truth." (Psalm 119:142)

Thanking you Father for who you are. You are the true and living God, the Most High God, the LORD God Almighty, my King and Master. I'm a slave to you and only you. I praise you dear Jesus, precious One of God, glorious and majestic. I reverence you in all your holiness and glory. My soul is overwhelmed because of your awesomeness and your presence. Help your servant to abide in you, knowing you will abide in me as well. Your word teaches that whoever abides in you and you in them will bear much fruit. Jesus, you are the core, the source, the root that feeds me, connect me and help me grow to fruitfulness. Without you I am just dried up and fruitless.

Dwell in me Jesus, take up residence in me. Make your address my heart and I want to dwell in you and make you my home. Without you I can do nothing. Let me be fruitful in all these things (i.e. love, growth, fruitfulness, answered prayers, glorifying God, forgiveness, tender-heartedness, self-control, gentleness, brotherly love, patience, joy, peace, goodness, and faithfulness).

My attention is towards heaven with you at the front of my thoughts. I feel you strengthening me with hinds' feet. I know my strength comes from you. I draw on all the strength, hope and purpose for you have given me a way out. My life and joy are in you, Jesus! Help me eat the words of life that I may see, listen and learn from the Holy Spirit, my Teacher. The most important knowledge to me is the knowledge of God the Father and the Lord Jesus Christ. I want to be known by you. I have nothing to hide from you. Search me Lord and know me. I want to be prepared for what you have planned for my life. Lead me and guide in all your ways because your way is perfect and upright. I want to follow you and be your disciple knowing it will cost me. Amen!

Encompassed by His Presence

*"Yahweh's Spirit will rest on him: the spirit of wisdom and understanding, the spirit of counsel and might, the spirit of knowledge and of the fear of Yahweh." **(Isaiah 11:2)***

love your word and I love your Spirit. Anoint me with continued revelation of your Word. Teach me to fear your name because I delight in the fear of the LORD. Help me to be a disciplined servant and student. I submit to your process so that I will be changed into your likeness and image. As I submit to Christ, allow Him to work in me and let me gain insights in His reality. I want a hunger and thirst for more knowledge of you that I may have spiritual vitality and wholeness.

I need you Lord even now, in this very moment. I don't want to go a second without having you on my mind. My very breathe depends on you. So glad you will never leave me nor forsake me. And if I remain in you, you will remain in me. I'm totally yours.

I close my eyes and sense the overwhelming presence of my Lord. I love you Jesus. I love being in your presence. Tell me what to do. I listen to hear you speaking to me. I love these gentle whispers that come even when I am in a crowd. Even now I feel faint from within because I am so in awe of you.

Mary J. Bryant

The Lord is My Delight

"Also delight yourself in Yahweh, and he will give you the desires of your heart." (Psalm 37:4)

Abba, Father, I cry holy, holy, holy to your name. Let your kingdom come; your will be done on earth as it is in heaven. You choice for me; you decide for me according to your perfect will, for I believe you are God: the Father, the Son, and the Holy Ghost. Reward me with your presence. Above all else Father, I seek to please you as Jesus did. You were always pleased with Him. I want to please you in all I do. It is my utmost desire to be in close communion with you daily.

I have no righteousness of my own and my confidence is not in myself. You have covered me with your righteousness by your blood that was shed on the cross and by your resurrection. My confidence is in you and you alone. I depend on you every step of the way for everything great and small. I want to please you, Father. I want to make you smile because I please you. Let me be like David and be a woman after your heart. Oh how I love you because you first love me. I choose you because you chose me.

I will be still and wait on you, because you are God, the Lord my Shepherd. I love your Word because "every word of yours is pure" (Proverbs 30:5). It cleanses my heart.

My spirit is energized from your Word, your Truth!

Somewhere Listening for His Voice

*"Happy are those who hear the joyful call to worship, for
they will walk in the light of your presence, LORD."*
(Psalm 89:15 NLT)

*"I have told you these things, that in me you may have
peace. In the world you have oppression; but cheer up! I have
overcome the world."* **(John 16:33)**

ather, I come again to say thank you and
acknowledge your holy name. I do, in your
presence, honor and worship you. I am in
awe of you! My faith teaches me that you are my Abba, Father. I
have been adopted into your family as your child. Therefore, I
approach you as such.

I love your perfect way, your life-giving, life-changing,
soul-stirring Word. They are indeed sweeter than the
honeycomb. Thank you! I am so grateful to you! I put my trust in
you. I depend on you and no longer depend on me and my
efforts. Your strength is made perfect in my weakness. You are
my creator and my master. You know the direction I should go. I
submit myself to you. I make your plans my plans, your purpose
my purpose, your will my will. Whatever you would have me do
or say, I am your yielded and willing vessel. I surrender with the
complete confidence that you will supply whatever it is that I
need to succeed to bring you glory and praise. Oh I bless your
holy name!

Sweet, wonderful Jesus! I feel such worship and
adoration in my spirit, even in the depths of my inner most
being. I can sense myself and in your presence; such love I am
basking in. I am humbled to be able to get to this place in you,
where the fellowship and communion with the God-Head is so
sweet and gentle, yet so intense. It overwhelms me. My soul
erupts with such joy and peace. I hunger and thirst for more of

you. Hallelujah! Glory to Your name, Oh Most High God!

I can't imagine my life without you. Where would I be if you, the LORD of Hosts, wasn't on my side. If the King of Glory wasn't for me, oh where would I be? So I offer up praise and thanksgiving for your shed blood and your resurrection.

Now how do I convey and share your goodness to others? I know you have a plan for me to be a laborer that is sent into the harvest. I can't seem to shake it or stop thinking about it. I dreamed of seeing myself standing behind a podium. I asked, "Why do I keep dreaming about such thing?" I am patient, watchful and prayerful to hear your voice for instructions and guidance.

Oh how I love our Precious Moments!

*"I will make you my wife forever, showing
you righteousness and justice, unfailing
love and compassion. I will be faithful to
you and make you mine, and you will
finally know me as LORD."*
Hosea 2:19-20

www.ingramcontent.com/pod-product-compliance
Lightning Source LLC
Chambersburg PA
CBHW030652110726
47901CB00002B/688